STOP BEING LAZY

GET OFF YOUR LAZY ASS!

You Are What You Do Every Single Second

Russell Hunter

Table of Contents

Chapter 1: *Reflect On Your Goals* 6
Chapter 2: Improving Your Sleeping Habits 9
Chapter 3: Importance Of Goal Setting 12
Chapter 4: How To Stop Getting In Your Own Way 16
Chapter 5: How To Achieve Deep Focus 20
Chapter 6: Five Ways To Stop Negative Spirals 24
Chapter 7: 8 Ways For Stress Relief 28
Chapter 8: 6 Signs Your Mental Health is Getting Worse 32
Chapter 9: 8 Bad Habits That Make You Age Faster 37
Chapter 10: 10 Habits Of Happy People 41
Chapter 11: 10 Habits of Ma Huateng 46
Chapter 12: 11 Hidden Signs of Borderline Personality Disorder 52
Chapter 13: Five Inspiration Pillars For Men 57
Chapter 14: Five Ways Of Dealing With A Health Crisis 61
Chapter 15: How To Deal with Loss (People) 65
Chapter 16: How to achieve true forgiveness? 69
Chapter 17: Five Ways to Tell if an Introvert is Mad at You. 73
Chapter 18: 8 Best Things To Do In Your Free Time 76
Chapter 19: Six Ways To Stop Procrastinating 80
Chapter 20: Stop Overthinking 84
Chapter 21: Ten Life Principles To Follow 88
Chapter 22: Ten psychological lessons not taught in school. 92
Chapter 23: Ten ways to become mentally stronger. 96
Chapter 24: Ten Ways To Make This Your Best Year 101
Chapter 25: The Psychology of Money 105
Chapter 26: Mindfulness Over Anxiety 109
Chapter 27: How Volunteering Can Make You Happy 113
Chapter 28: How To Stop Worrying and Go To Sleep 116

Chapter 29: How to Persuade People Effortlessly.................................... 119
Chapter 30: Five things that destroy the first impression immediately
.... 123
Chapter 31: 10 Habits Of The Sigma Male... 127
Chapter 32: Five Ways To Rid Yourself Of Distraction........................ 132
Chapter 33: How To Deal With Stress (For Women)........................... 136
Chapter 34: 5 Signs You Are Smarter Than Most People 140

Chapter 1:
Reflect On Your Goals

A good place to start is to look back at the short-term goals you set at the start of the year, as well as the longer-term goals you have for your career. Are you happy with the progress you've made so far towards achieving these goals? It's okay if you're struggling. Only 9% of people achieve their new year's resolutions, whether that's to get fit, kick a bad habit, or make real career progress.

While your goals may be clear in your mind, maintaining your progress is not always easy. How can you keep yourself on track? Here are some strategies to help.

Try the SMART technique

Ask yourself:

- is my goal Specific?
- is my goal Measurable?
- is my goal ultimately Achievable?
- is it Relevant to my values?
- is my goal Time-bound?

Using this method gives you clarity and detail on what your goal is and helps you track your progress toward it.

Know your sub-goals may change

The sub-goals you planned and the route to achieving your main goal may change along the way. That's okay – plans change. Don't be put off; it doesn't mean your end goal isn't achievable, it means you might need to take another path to get there. If you consistently miss your sub-goals, consider a new route – or whether or not the end goal is still right for you and your career.

Be accountable

Hold yourself to account for achieving your goals by announcing them to others. Doing this also makes goals feel more 'real'. Start conversations about your goals with friends, peers or colleagues, so they can check in with your progress.

Change Your Habits

If you find yourself stuck turning your goals into actions, try Moodnotes or the WOOP app (Wish, Outcome, Obstacle, Plan). Use these to form proactive goal-setting habits and observe your progress, so you can overcome barriers and stay on track.

Be Aware Of Your Edge Behaviours

An edge behaviour is an emotional, physical or mental behaviour you experience as you come up against change, uncertainty or growth. An example of this could be procrastination, or telling yourself you're not good enough. Being aware of how your behaviours shift is important because they impact your mood and your ability to move forward.

Check in with your edge behaviours by recording, assessing and adjusting them so that you can adapt to change effectively.

Track And Celebrate Your Successes

It's important to celebrate small wins because these incremental achievements help you stay excited about your goals. Every time you achieve something - no matter how small - write it down or make a note in your phone or planner. When you're feeling unmotivated, go through these previous successes to get perspective and boost your morale.

Chapter 2:
Improving Your Sleeping Habits

Sleeping habits are an important part of growth. It is sad how most people have degraded sleep and it has turned out to be a measure of laziness. If you truly want to know the importance of sleep, deprive yourself of it for a few days and watch how your body will respond.

The importance of sleep cannot be over-emphasized. Have you noticed how fresh and strong you feel after waking up from a long and satisfying sleep? It is not the short naps and siestas during the day but the total rest that you get at night. You should constantly improve your sleeping habits. There are bad sleeping habits as well as good ones. Here is a whole list about them and how they can be remedied:

1. Sleeping Late

Pushing daytime tasks into the night will not make you perform any better. Sometimes you may find yourself sleeping late because you did not realize time flies as you were storytelling. This is not enough justification. The remedy to sleeping late is developing a sleep schedule with consistent times to go to bed and wake up. Healthy sleep should be at least 8 hours long and uninterrupted. Depending on what time you want to wake up, observe bedtime time.

2. Sleeping With Tight Clothes

Some people sleep in tight clothes at night. This is unhealthy because sleep is a time of rest and your body should feel free. Comfort during sleep is important. The remedy to sleeping in tight clothes is having nightclothes – a night dress or pajamas. They are highly recommended because they are tailored to factor in comfort during sleep. Do not sleep in jeans or clothes that you had during the day.

3. Constantly Checking Your Phone When You Go To Bed

Most 'modern' people are guilty of this crime – addiction to mobile phones. They carry their phones when going to bed (which is okay) but misuse them in bed. The misuse is that they start checking their social media and browser feeds when it is bedtime. The remedy to this misuse of mobile phones and other electronics is putting them aside when going to bed. This is not enough. Switch your phone to silent mode or turn on do not disturb (DND). Continued phone notifications will interrupt your sleep.

4. Listening To Music As You Sleep

The habit of listening to music on your earphones or speaker when you have gone to bed is unhealthy. Music may soothe you into sleep at the beginning but it is a distraction that many people love. No matter how loveable it is, loud music will deprive you of sleep. The remedy to listening to music in bed is that you do not use your earphones and lower the volume when playing on the speaker. Soft music will make you fall asleep. You can also set the music to switch off after about one hour or so because you would have fallen asleep already.

5. Oversleeping

Sleeping is good but too much of it is unhealthy. Sleep must be regulated. You should neither go to bed late nor wake up late. Find a balance between the two and you shall optimize the importance of sleep. The remedy to oversleeping is setting an alarm. It will help you wake up early and as well as observe your sleeping schedule. Alarms are noisy and you should check-up with your roommate if they are comfortable with it (especially if it goes off early in the morning).

Conclusion

Sleep is important for your well-being. Great sleeping habits will make you sleep better and healthier. Observe the remedies to these five bad sleeping habits to be on the safe side.

Chapter 3
Importance Of Goal Setting

Goals And Scores

Goals are targets set to be achieved. They are an important part of progress. In fact, your progress is measured by whether or not you have achieved your goals or if you are closer to them.

Maybe the term goal was coined from the soccer game rules. A team has to score a goal to win the match. Likewise, wins in life are measured by how many of your set goals you have achieved.

Everyone has goals. Families, society, and even the country. Without them, our progress is blind. But why is setting goals overrated?

It is overrated because the absence of goals is a recipe for failure. You will have nothing to look forward to. Here are five major important reasons for setting goals:

1. Keeping You Focused

Goals will keep you on your toes. They willgive you a reason to be on track with your projects. This is the reason why we set goals for ourselves or set standards for minors.

To some, the fear of failure is what keeps them on their toes. Failure is defined by the inability to meet set goals. This is clearly demonstrated in learning institutions. The school management, with the help of learners, comes up with a class target mean score annually. The idea is for one class to perform better than its predecessor.

The target will be achieved by the cumulative efforts of all stakeholders. Whenever issues come up at school, they will be reminded about their target mean score. Everybody resumes working towards the target.

That is the focus that goal setting inspires.

2. To Develop A Working Plan

It is said that a good plan is a job half done. When you have set a goal of achieving a certain target within a specified duration, what follows is developing a mechanism to make that possible. You cannot plan blindly.

A goal gives you a framework on how you can plan. There are many variables in meeting the target that will be unforeseen without a solid goal in place. In your plan, you can take care of what threatens the success of meeting your goal.

While still considering the example of goal setting in learning institutions, how do they work around meeting their target? It is after agreeing on the goal (target mean score) that they get to develop a working plan to achieve it.

A goal is a fundamental part of a working plan.

3. A Source Of Motivation

We draw our inspiration from our goals. In the first place, there is a reason why we set that goal. We were inspired to reach that particular level. The motivation to beat a mean score set by the last class of a national examination is what makes the next class set a higher target mean score.

The bar keeps moving higher with each successive examination lot. Goal-setting becomes a great source of motivation. We are continuously motivated by the desire to be better as measured by our goals.

Nothing should separate you from the sweet victory that lies ahead.

4. You Can Know When You Stray

Goals are like a destination. When you take a different route from where your destination is, you are definitely lost. Your distance and route from your destination determine when you will arrive if at all you will.

Goals help you to stay on track as you work towards achieving them. Without them, it is difficult to tell whether or not you are on the right track.

5. You Can Use Your Resources Optimally

There are always limited resources that we are likely to misuse when we are still guessing our way around life. This is all the more reason why we must figure out what we want to do with our lives and set personal goals for ourselves.

Goal setting allows you to use the available resources wisely. Everything will be for the greater good of the future.

The importance of goal setting cannot be overemphasized. These five reasons are enough reasons why you should consider it before it is too late.

Chapter 4:

How To Stop Getting In Your Own Way

Are there valid reasons why you can't get things done? Absolutely. In fact, many times, external forces are working against you — think a sick child, flat tire, or global pandemic. There are, however, times when it turns out that we're our own biggest obstacle. We also call this self-sabotage. And, it can be brutal when it comes to productivity and our wellbeing. The good news? You can conquer this by getting out of your way. And, it's feasible by trying out the following techniques.

Remember your why

Instead of going through the motions and doing things for no reason, reconnect with your purpose. If you can't connect the dots between the activity and the big picture, then stop doing it. That doesn't mean avoiding tasks that you don't always enjoy. For example, as a new business owner, you might dread bookkeeping. However, it's an essential responsibility if you want your business to thrive. Remind yourself that maintaining your finances, sticking to a budget, and preparing your taxes can help you reach your business goals. And, as your business scales up, you can eventually hand this off to someone else.

Acknowledge your strengths

A strength is an activity that strengthens you. It doesn't have to be something that you excel at. Instead, it's something that you look forward to and "leaves you feeling energized. A strength is more appetite than ability, and it's that appetite that drives us to want to do it again; practice more; refine it to perfection. The appetite leads to the practice, which leads to performance.Leveraging your strengths and managing around your weaknesses isn't just about making yourself feel better. It's about conditioning yourself to contribute the best of yourself every day. It's about performance.

Nothing compares to you — except you

You bust your tail but aren't as productive as a colleague. You see that a friend just bought a new car or are enjoying a luxurious vacation. And, that just leaves you feeling like a failure.But, as Mark Twain once said, "comparison is the death of joy."Research backs that statement up. Comparing yourself to others leads to low self-confidence and depression. It can also make you green with envy, deplete motivation, and doesn't bring you closer to your goals.In short, if you measure yourself against others, you're always going to come short. Instead, practice gratitude. And, better yet, compare yourself by tracking your progress and celebrating what you've accomplished.

Run with the right crowd

Are you familiar with saying, "you are what you eat?" "Well, it's also true when it comes to who you keep company with. You may not realize this. But, the people you interact with on a daily basis directly influence who you are and what you do. Make sure you surround yourself with people who encourage you and hold you accountable—people from who you can learn positive habits from.

Remove unnecessary pressure

Life is hectic enough. So, why make things worse by overcommitting or setting unrealistic expectations?Be realistic about what you can actually accomplish. If you don't have the availability or skillset, just say "no." For example, if you're calendar is already packed, decline time requests like unnecessary meetings or talking to a friend on the phone for two hours.

Engage in self-care

Some might consider self-care as a selfish act. In reality, it's making time for activities that leave you feeling calm and energized. These are vital in supporting your mental, physical, and emotional wellbeing.Examples can include going for a walk, journaling, hobbies, meditating, or taking a shower. Since time might appear to be a concern, add self-care to your calendar. For instance, you could leave an hour blank from 1 pm to 2 pm to spend however you like.

Avoid ruminating

Ruminating is a cycle of repeating thoughts that you just can't shake. As a result, this can impair thinking and problem-solving. And, it can cause you to get stuck in your own head. To break free of these swirling thoughts, distract yourself. Examples are doing chores, reading, or calling a friend. You can also question your beliefs, set more attainable goals, and take small action steps to solve problems.

Chapter 5:

How To Achieve Deep Focus

Deep Focus Or Focus Deep?

The former is just a statement while the second one is imperative. Choose the imperative. It is almost becoming mandatory to focus deep on everything or you may be shortchanged when you least expect it. However, the deep focus has been elusive for many.

Its importance is the pillar that holds your life. You may probably not know it, but it is the reason why you have been successfully implementing your plans. There is more in deep focus apart from successfully executing your plans.

1. Reaching Your Potential

Deep focus allows you to maximize your potential. This is because you channel all your energy to one specific cause. You can accomplish what initially took you days within hours if you focus deeply on it. This is the glory of deep focus.

If you recall correctly, you reached the highest moment of your life when you started paying attention to the details at hand. You expended all your energy and resources on one subject and it eventually paid off.

2. New Discoveries

It is not about new discoveries of third parties but about yourself. Deep focus makes that possible. When you practice it frequently, your new traits show up.

Subjecting yourself to a deep focus on one thing at a time will make your mind adapt to this new strategy. You become mentally strong and resilient to what could initially freak you out. Is this not what we all want?

Yes, the deep focus is achievable. Here is a four-step guide to it:

1. Be In A Calm Environment

Deep focus can be reached in a calm environment. Tranquility gives the mind peace and relaxation. Speaking in a calm environment is like speaking to yourself. You can literally converse with yourself there.

No wonder examination halls are some of the quietest places. It is for students to maximize their ability to recall as they write their exams. There should be no excuse for failing. Hospitals too are very quiet places except for the occasional groaning by patients in pain.

The secret to tranquility is to provide a conducive environment for people to focus deeply on what they should. The human mind relates sounds to past experiences. This will interrupt the process of deep focus.

2. Train Your Mind On One Subject

You cannot afford to think about multiple things if you want to achieve deep focus. Concentration is like a Christian monogamous marriage. You can only get 'married' to one thought at a time.

Considering Christianity, it is a sin to be in marriage and covet other partners. Deep focus follows this principle. You should choose to train your mind on one thing and brainstorm it entirely to exhaustion. You will void your deep focus moment if you wander from one thought to another. It is imperative to be faithful.

Once you conceive a thought, delve into it entirely. Pick one at a time. There is no turning back once you are in your moment of deep focus.

3. Learn To Travel Through Time

Time-traveling or teleporting is a fantasy in movies. The good news is that deep focus makes it a reality. When you are concentrating on one subject, you literally migrate from this world to another one.

This helps you achieve deep focus faster because you think of the future without interruption by anything in the present. Getting into deep focus widens the scope of your thoughts. You can even consider some variables that you were blind to if you do not travel through time.

4. Withdrawal

Withdrawing from deep thought is not easy especially if you are fantasizing about your beautiful future. It is a beautiful moment to behold and escape from your present troubles.

However, how you stop deep focus affects how soon you can resume. You should not be shocked back to reality. The transition should be smooth.

You can easily switch from deep focus to your world. This is the epitome of deep focus.

Much can be achieved in deep focus if only you master how to achieve it and how to transit back to normalcy. Think tanks know this secret so well.

Chapter 6:

Five Ways To Stop Negative Spirals

What Are They?

Negative spirals are dreaded by many. You cannot even wish it upon your enemy. But what really are they? They are a swarm of bad thoughts that 'attack' you when you least expect them.

Their effects have far and wide-reaching complications. Negative spirals are not a respecter of persons or status. It does not spare even the King!

Can you imagine when you are driving on a highway and you suddenly remember a grisly road accident you were involved in? You will definitely lose control and cause yet another accident. This is what negative spirals can do if you do not stop them on time. Here is how:

1. Strive Not To Be Alone

There are times when you need to be alone. But where do you draw the line between being alone and being lonely?

Self-withdrawal is good because you have the time for self-reflection. You can achieve much because with no external influence, you can come back to your senses if you had strayed.

However, you attract negative spirals when you are alone. Most of the time you think about the worst happening to you is when you are alone. It is important to often be with people who will engage you in conversations.

Talking about diverse topics will occupy your mind and not entertain any negative spirals. The mind cannot be empty. Something must occupy it. Choose to be among people and talk with them.

2. Interact With Good News

Do you know that no news is good news? This is to say that it is better not to know anything than to know the bad news. As much as there is a lot of unavoidable things, you have control over a majority of them. You cannot choose what you hear but you can decide what to listen to.

Negative spirals thrive in bad news. The more you listen to them, the more they take root in your mind. Your perception of many things depends on your interaction with good or bad news.

3. Change Your Environment

It is not enough to try to move on if you still stay in the same environment with bad memories. You need to move to new places that will encourage you to forget about the past.

Negative spirals are provoked by places with bad memories. One negative thought attracts another and they build up to occupy your mind. They may cause you to suffer from anxiety that can harm your health.

After changing your environment, start to make new memories that will slowly replace the old ones. Make it intentional to have fun and erase the hurtful moments of the past. Negative spirals will keep you away from you because they no longer relate to you in any way.

4. Engage In Philosophy Or Religion

It is good to have something you believe in – be it religion or philosophy. Either of them provides strong beliefs that will take your mind off negative spirals.

Philosophy or religion gives you a chance to believe in the supernatural. It is important to believe in a higher being or authority that will assure you of a better future. It may not be true that either of them can make your worries go away, but they sure can keep your mind on the right track.

Negative spirals cannothave space in a fortified mind. Both philosophy and religion prepare you for rough patches of life. Like muscles that get stronger with practice, so does your spirit get stronger with teachings of philosophy and religion?

5. Confess Positivity

Positive confession is not living in denial. It is important to be optimistic if at all you want to keep at bay negative spirals.

Practice confessing victory anytime regardless of any difficulty you may face. Negative spirals are entertained by words of doom. They are the fodder that is fed upon by negativity.

Stopping negative spirals is what we would like. It is insufficient to simply wish a good life for yourself. Implement these five ways to stop negative spirals.

Chapter 7:

8 Ways For Stress Relief

From minor to major issues, stress is naturally part of life. Even when the current circumstances have highlighted the rising stress levels, the phenomenon is not new. And while you may have no control over your circumstances, you control how you react to them. Stress can gravely take a toll on your overall health if it becomes chronic or overwhelming. In fact, according to a study that was conducted in 2012, unmanaged daily stress increases the likelihood of developing chronic health problems 10 years down the road.

So, is stress becoming more infuriating and upsetting? Is it affecting your mental peace and overall healthy? Relieving your daily stress is the most pleasing way of restoring serenity and calmness. Simply put, resort to the following easy, and proven stress relief techniques.

Here are 8 ways for stress relief.

1. Log Off, Stay Unplugged

Relieving stress is possible by simply pressing the "turn off" button on your phone. In the same efforts you put to control your diet, do the same to your social media interactions especially in the first hour of your day. Take command of the first hour by clearing your mind, setting motives, stretching, and hydrating. Doing so allows you to gain clarity and control of the entire day.

2. Take Charge

One of the primary causes of stress is losing control over one's circumstances. Taking control is an empowering act in and of itself, and it's a necessary step toward finding a solution that calms you down. Every issue has a solution. And if you remain passive, blaming yourself for being in that situation, you are in for the worst.

3. Exercise

Although exercising cannot erase all your stressful thoughts permanently, it will help you relieve the intensity and thus allowing you to handle the problems more calmly. In a recent Medicine and Science in sports and exercise journal, exercising is found to be the most accurate and healthy way of dealing or relieving stress. The journal suggests moderate physical exercises like running, dancing, and spinning as stress relievers.

4. Resort to Healthy Drinking and Eating Lifestyle

To cope with stress, we frequently turn to excessive alcohol or overeating. Yes, these habits are relaxing in the short term, but they increase stress in the long haul. Furthermore, they will degrade your health. Instead, resort to a healthy eating and drinking plan.

5. Try Something New

Establishing new goals or challenging yourself, such as learning a foreign language, volunteering, or participating in a sport, can enable you to build confidence. You also lower or relieve tension while participating in such activities. Continued learning makes you a more emotionally resilient person. It equips you with knowledge and motivates you to act rather than sit back and just do nothing.

6. Leave the Work-Life at Your Office

A person who can leave their professional life at the office to savor their personal life can effectively deal with daily stress. Strike a work-life balance and mindset whereby both are adding value to your life. Don't be a person whose career defines who you are.

7. Accept Change

Change is never easy to accept or incorporate into one's daily life. And changing a problematic situation that you've found yourself in isn't easy. However, to move forward positively and avoid becoming entangled in that situation, you must accept change. The goal is to avoid wasting time on things that drain your energy and make you unhappy because you need to be productive and add value to your life. Just prioritize things you are in control of and leave the rest to Mother Nature.

8. Laugh More Often

Having a moment where you feel a good sense of humor won't take your pain away, but it will make you feel better. Laughter alleviates stress and causes profound positive effects on the body. It stimulates and deactivates the stress response. So, you can embark to good Netflix comedies, or hang out with funny friends.

Conclusion

Life is full of inevitable ups and downs, and it's all normal to experience stress at all walks of your life. To maintain your sanity, you'll need to bring down stress to a manageable level. Apply the above stress relief strategies at every stage of your life.

Chapter 8:

6 Signs Your Mental Health is Getting Worse

If you typically have mild or intermittent depression symptoms, you might notice immediately if they suddenly become more severe or persistent.Still, the different types of depression can involve a range of symptoms, and changes might creep up slowly instead of falling on you all at once.You might not always recognize small but steady changes in your day-to-day mood until you suddenly feel a whole lot worse than you usually do.

If any of the following signs sound familiar, it's worth talking to your primary care doctor, therapist, or another healthcare professional about a new approach to treatment. If you haven't yet started treatment for depression, talking to a therapist about these symptoms is a good next step.

1. Almost Nothing Sparks Your Interest

Depression commonly involves a decrease in your energy levels and a loss of pleasure in your favourite hobbies and other things you usually enjoy. As you work toward recovery, you'll usually find your interest in these activities slowly begins to return, along with your energy.

2. With Worsening Depression, You Might Notice The Opposite

It may not just seem difficult to find the motivation for exercise, socializing, and other hobbies. Anhedonia, or difficulty experiencing joy and pleasure, is a core symptom of depression.

You might also have trouble mustering up enough energy to go to work or take care of basic responsibilities, like paying bills or preparing meals. Even necessary self-care, like showering and brushing your teeth, might feel beyond your current abilities.

3. You Spend More Time Alone

With depression, you might find it challenging to enjoy the company of others for a number of reasons. You may not feel up to socializing simply because you have less energy. Emotional numbness can make the social interactions you usually enjoy seem pointless.

Feelings of guilt, irritability, or worthlessness can also complicate your mood and make avoidance seem like the safer option. There's nothing wrong with spending time alone when you enjoy it. An increasing sense of loneliness, on the other hand, can make your mood even worse. You might begin to feel as if no one understands or cares about your experience.

4. Your Mood Gets Worse At Certain Times Of Day

Changes in how you experience symptoms might also suggest worsening depression. Your symptoms may have previously remained mostly stable throughout the day. Now, you notice they intensify in the morning or evening. Or perhaps they feel much worse on some days instead of remaining fairly consistent from day to day.

5. You Notice Changes In Eating And Sleeping Patterns

Depression often affects appetite and sleep habits. When it comes to appetite changes, you might find yourself eating more than usual. You could also lose your appetite entirely and feel as if you have to force yourself to eat.

Sleep changes often happen on a similar spectrum. You could have a hard time staying awake and feel exhausted enough to sleep all day — but you could also struggle to fall asleep or wake up often throughout the night. Trouble sleeping at night can mean you need to nap during the day to catch up, so you might end up drifting off at unusual times. This can affect your energy and concentration and further disrupt your sleep.

6. Intensifying Emotional Distress

If you have depression, you'll likely notice the following:
- hopelessness
- sadness
- a pessimistic outlook or catastrophic thinking
- feelings of guilt, shame, or worthlessness
- a sense of numbness
- problems with concentration or memory
- These feelings sometimes increase over time, so you might find yourself:
- fixating on negative thoughts
- worrying what others think of you or believing loved ones consider you a burden
- crying more often
- considering self-harm as a way to ease distress or numbness
- having frequent thoughts of suicide, even if you don't intend to act on them

If this distress persists or continues to get worse even with treatment, connect with a healthcare professional right away. It's not unusual for mental health symptoms to fluctuate over time. These changes may not always have a clear cause. Sometimes, though, they happen in response to specific triggers.

A few factors that could help explain worsening depression symptoms include:

- Stress
- Your treatment plan
- A different mental health condition
- Medication side effects
- Substance use

Chapter 9:

8 Bad Habits That Make You Age Faster

According to a statistic given in an article in Globe Newswire, it's projected that by the year 2019, the global anti-aging market will be worth 191.7 billion dollars! Clearly, a lot of people are investing in products and procedures to help keep themselves looking young and beautiful. But, as with any disease or condition, prevention is always far better than the cure, and the same holds true for anti-aging. Unfortunately, there is no magic fountain of youth that will keep you young forever. But there are some particular habits and mistakes that, when avoided, can make you less likely to need anti-aging products and procedures. If you're a person who is concerned about an aging appearance, it's going to be important to avoid the things that make you age faster!

1. Processed Foods

Foods that have been highly processed and refined not only lack the nutrients needed by the body to support proper functioning, they typically also contain synthetic chemicals and other harmful ingredients that are detrimental to health. These processed foods cause faster tissue breakdown and other cellular damage that leads to faster aging.

Additionally, when the nutrients that the bodily tissues need to function optimally are not optimally supplied, both the function and appearance of the skin and other organs can suffer.

2. Smoking

Smoking is a habit that not only wreaks havoc on your health but certainly speeds up the aging process. Even smoking one cigarette causes a huge amount of oxidative stress. This oxidative stress causes wear and tear on the body's cells, causing many issues such as aging, wrinkles, and other forms of degeneration.

3. Drug Abuse

Too much drug use of any kind causes internal stress on the body that again causes dysfunction, breakdown, and lack of optimal functioning. Depending on the drug, some can cause water loss, loss of healthy fat tissue, toxicity and more that can leave you looking older and frailer.

4. Lack Of Hydration

Being improperly hydrated, especially chronically, surprisingly can make you look more aged. Water is essential for so many roles in the body that without enough of it, the function of the body suffers, which both directly and indirectly, can lead to quicker aging. Water gives your skin the soft, plump, vibrant, moist look that indicates health and youthfulness. Additionally, it helps internally to flush out toxins that can cause acne, red eyes, bags under the eyes, puffiness, and other ailments that certainly don't scream youthfulness!

5. Not Getting Enough Sleep

Getting insufficient sleep is a major way to age yourself quite quickly! A chronic lack of sleep causes the body to shut down. Your eyes become bloodshot and red, baggy eyes, wrinkled skin, low energy, and many other symptoms that make anyone look older than they are! Sleep is so important both for health and for beauty that there's even the common saying, "I need my beauty sleep!"

6. Stress

Being chronically stressed is another habit that wreaks havoc internally. Stress typically is also associated with other habits that hasten the aging process. When stressed, people tend to sleep more poorly, eat more poorly, take more medications and drugs, and other such things that disrupt health and advance aging. Chronic stress keeps stress hormones elevated in the bloodstream constantly, which can have negative effects on the complexion of your skin, both the coloration and wrinkles, and causes red eyes, and an overall slumped, broken down and aged function and appearance. Having these stress hormones elevated chronically can lead to a number of health problems, the least of which is wrinkles and aging!

7. Being Physically Inactive

Being inactive is a sure way of making your body look and feel older than it really is. Sedentary living typically causes you to have poor posture, become overweight, lethargic, and just plain droopy! Keeping your body moving and strong does a surprising amount for keeping you looking and feeling youthful from the inside out. Individuals who stay active as they get older typically age much better.

8. Prolonged Exposure To UV Rays

Getting too much exposure to UV rays, either from being out in the sun unprotected too much or from tanning bed use, really causes a lot of damage to the skin, leading to wrinkles, sunspots and other damage that makes you look old.

By consistently maintaining a wholesome, natural, active lifestyle, you'll automatically be on a better track for avoiding fast aging. Following a diet of fresh, natural foods, being active, managing stress, and getting proper sleep can do leaps and bounds for helping you stay youthful!

Chapter 10:

10 Habits Of Happy People

Happiness is a state of joy. In happiness, one is thrilled, contented, and tickled by joy. It is often expressed through bursts of laughter amidst smiles and it cannot be hidden. Happiness is a state everyone desires but few can maintain. Here are ten habits of happy people:

1. They Are Outgoing

Happy people are very social. They easily interact with strangers and make friends faster than ordinary people. They are charming to a fault and you cannot help but love their company.

Happy people are easily noticeable in a room full of different people. They are conspicuously outgoing to initiate trips, vacations, and team-building activities. Their social nature makes them thrive both in outdoor and indoor interactions.

2. They Are Self-Driven

Happy people have a strong personality that drives them in life. They are not coerced to do something and often act out of self-will. They stand out from a population that requires much convincing before they act.

They live a purposeful life that is crystal in their minds. Happy people do not need an external influence to be happy. They genuinely derive pleasure from what they do.

3. They Wake Up Early

Happy people know the secret of waking up early and do not need persuasion to wake up earlier than everybody else.
In waking up early, they keep off conflict with other people who could ruin their day. They build the foundation of the day ahead of them in the morning and they can maintain the tempo until the end. Strangers can do very little to ruin their happiness.

4. They Are Positive About Life

Happy people are very optimistic about life. Positivity is their middle name. They hardly entertain thoughts of failure. Like all of us, happiness is a choice they have to constantly make and work towards it. It distinguishes them from everyone else.
How can you be happy if you do not see the good out of the ugly? Happy people look at the brighter side of life because the grass is not greener on the other side but where you water it.

5. They Keep The Company Of Other Happy People

Happy people keep the fire of happiness burning because they associate with like-minded people. They share ideas and strategies on how to pursue their purpose. They also encourage each other when hope is bleak.

The company of sad and angry people is devastating because it gives no room for happiness to thrive. Happy people embrace each other's company because it is all they have got if they are to stay happy.

6. They Read Success Stories

Success stories are inspiring. They make us pull our socks and give us hope to succeed as others have. Happy people read and share success stories because therein lies happiness. They bask in the glory of their friends because they believe their turn too shall come.

Happy people shunbad news and stories of despair because they are discouraging and one could succumb to depression if they are not careful.

7. They Know How To Handle Bad News And Rejection

Happy people know that rejection does not spell doom for them. They have hope that they can rise above all challenges they face and still be happy. Unlike ordinary people who take rejection personally and despair, happy people consider it as another phase of life.

Handling bad news is a skill that happy people have perfected. Although some bad news could hit them hard, they know how to soak in their happiness and not live in sadness.

8. They Are Agents Of Change

Happy people are agents of change wherever they go. They make a difference with their speech and their aura changes everything. Everybody can feel the impact of happy people wherever they are.

Happy people inspire others to be like them. They recruit others in their league of happiness because they desire to see a changing world.

9. They Are Loving And Caring

Happy people can afford to be caring because they have no traces of bitterness or anger within them. They genuinely care for the welfare of other people.

Happiness makes people loving unlike those who harbor anger. You can only give what you have and it is natural for happy people to care more and sad people hurt more.

10. They Live An Authentic Lifestyle

Authenticity is a mark of happy people. They live a genuine lifestyle without seeking to impress anyone. Their joy does not lie in the approval of strangers but the satisfaction of their needs.

Happy people live within their financial means and not in the standards that other people have put for them. Their priorities are independent of external influence.

In conclusion, happy people are easy to spot. It is everybody's dream to be happy but a very elusive one. These ten habits of happy people distinguish them from others.

Chapter 11:

10 Habits of Ma Huateng

Magnificent attach to Ma Gauteng, who also goes by the nickname "Pony Ma," a technology juggernaut, the founder and CEO of Tencent. Tencent is China's leading internet and innovation company and the largest entertainment and gaming conglomerate. Tencent is behind the messaging app "WeChat," with over 1 billion users owing to its mixed features of WhatsApp, Uber, Google News, and Deliveroofeature it.

While the pandemic may have inconvenienced everyone in one way or another, technology tycoons like Ma Hauteng hold a contrary thought. He is dominating china's richest rank, suppressing Jack Ma, founder, and owner of "Alibaba."How has he become this outstanding?

Here are 10 habits of Ma Hauteng.

1. Gauteng Keeps His Competitors Close

Nowadays, with all the competition out there, launching your new ideas or products is troublesome. You can't take a big piece of the pie because it's already divided up. However, in China, the contrary is that there is still hope. It's from such hope that Hauteng benefited after launching Tencent with different products and portfolios. China being a communist country, local products are favored, and thus when Hautenglaunched WeChat, videogames, everyone started using them because they were similar to Western apps. Why are they similar? Because Ma copies them, and more to it, he even bought shares in Tesla, Snapchat, and Spotify to spy a little more on his competitors.

2. Humble Beginning makes up for a successful business.

Gauteng Ma had a very humble beginning and a rough start in life. After graduating from college, he worked for a salary of not more than $176. First jobs, as you can see, are usually difficult; even billionaires can attest to that. You need to start from the bottom to appreciate it when you are at the top. For Ma, luckily, the company he built from scratch is worth more than any other in China, which is now battling for market shares and users with giant competitors.

3. He Struggles With Understanding the Customers

Gauteng may not have discovered social media, but sure he's involved in developing and improving it. When you develop a product used in everyone's daily life, you feel responsible when users use it maliciously, which was the case for Ma with WeChat a few times. Although Apps have so many tracking and reports, providing information about a user is hard. Ma has opened up severally that to date; he struggles with understanding how young people are, which keeps him awake at night.

4. Agility

Ma's business is founded on the ability to move swiftly and adapt quickly. How did he develop the ability to transform in anticipation of and respond to changes? By creating the right culture. At Tsinghua Management Global Forum, Pony Ma insisted that his desire to create "hot products" suppressed the focus on building a great enterprise, hence driving a transformative culture that required the ability to change a product in flight. Realizing how digitized the world is becoming will make you "Pony Ma" if you adapt to changes in your business.

5. Customers First

While carrying on your business, know that consumers, irrespective of their age or background, prefer clear, natural, and simple-to-use products or designs. With Tencent, that's a sure bet. Tencent has managed to combine as many features as possible in one app. Ma's 10/100/1000 rule entails and enforces a customer-friendly ideal, which is why product managers engage in an extensive survey through blogs and experience feedback from people.

6. Speed Is Essential in Tech-World

Nothing starts perfect, but you can have your product in utterance, and even as Ma says, "perfection may neverbereached."It takes rapid iteration speed to get ahead in the market. Tencent's focus on speed has long turned its competitors green. Through this, WeChat was able to outdo "Xiaomi's Chat App because even as Lei Jun admitted, "Tencent can release one or two versions every week, in contrast to his one-month margin speed.

7. Resilience

Gauteng's mission to deal with both internal and external competition includes being resilient. From an internal perspective, he understands the possibility of suffering waste, and from an external perspective, it's quite obvious that Ma is battling with giants like Facebook, Baidu, Amazon, Google, Alibaba. However, Ma believes in intolerance to failure and recovery after setbacks; thus, whenever you fail, pick yourself up and begin again as you develop a sense of tolerance to failure.

8. Open-mindedness

According to Gauteng, openness entails providing your employees with the freedom to perform, invent, problem-solve, and wow in their abilities. Gauteng adopted open-source software, allowing his employees to share insights, codes, and software from other industry segments. He always encourages his employees to try new things without fear, how WeChat came to be. As once his idol, Steve Jobs, said, "If you don't cannibalize yourself, someone else will."

9. Evolution

Gauteng describes evolution as the ability to create room for improvement, self-correct, and stay focused. Tencent came about before the mobile age but was able to move and adapt to time evolution demands. According to Ma, adding mobile internet is a revolutionary process that requires your speed and ability to adapt to progressive changes. WeChat's success is owed to its likeliness to WhatsApp and Kik, while QQ reigned supreme in the PC area and was later modified to suit mobile.

10. Hauteng Is Charitable

Charity is essential and beneficial, and when you look at some people's bank accounts, it seems obvious that they should be the first to undertake charity. A few donates huge sums as Hauteng Ma transferred his 2 billion dollars' worth of shares to his charitable foundations.

Conclusion

Ma Hauteng's success journey can also be your journey but only if you make his habits your habits too. And also as long as they fit your line of business. Just Like Ma, when you put on effort and work towards your goals, you'll definitely make a difference in your life.

Chapter 12:

11 Hidden Signs of Borderline Personality Disorder

Those who experience "hidden" manifestations of BPD symptoms are often called "quiet" borderlines. The term "quiet" BPD isn't an official diagnosis, but rather a term to describe someone with BPD who doesn't express their symptoms as obviously. For example, a person with quiet BPD might experience the same level of uncontrollable anger as a person with "typical" BPD, but instead of lashing out outwardly, they might direct their anger inwardly through constant negative self-talk or hidden self-harm.

Because BPD doesn't always present outwardly like we think it does, we wanted to shine light on the experiences of people with "quiet" BPD. Just because something isn't as visible doesn't mean it's any less painful to live with. We wanted to know what the "hidden signs" of quiet BPD so we are sharing some signs that typically go unnoticed

1. Self-Blame

Because people with BPD tend to feel more strongly than others, they experience emotions like guilt intensely. This can lead to chronic self-blame.

They usually blame themselves for a lot of things, even when it isn't there fault. And a lot of the time they think their friends could do better than them. They feel like they annoy them too much or they are too much trouble to bother with."

2. Mentally Retreating

When triggered, it's normal to retreat inward to protect yourself. If this is something you consistently struggle with, you're not alone.

Mentally retreating and feeling yourself go down the spiral, while being able to maintain a good outward appearance. Nobody notices the change… Having to deal with depression and anxiety along with your BPD. People think they are 'doing better' whereas they are just good at hiding the hard things.

3. Beating Yourself Up

Like we mentioned earlier, folks with quiet BPD often direct anger inward. This can lead to chronic negative self-talk. If you are struggling with negative self-talk, we encourage you to reach out to a therapist. Here's a handy tool for [finding a therapist in your area](#).

They internally attack themselves. Like a wolf attacking its prey, their mind rips them to shreds.

4. Being a People Pleaser

People-pleasing or "fawning" is a typical response to trauma. The majority of people with BPD have a history with trauma. In fact, in a recent study, researchers found BPD was the mental illness with the strongest link to childhood trauma.

5. Being Afraid Of Emotional Intimacy

Fear of abandonment can cause folks with quiet BPD to retreat from relationships entirely. Unfortunately, this leaves people without the support friends, family and partners can provide. Thankfully, many therapists specialize in relationship issues and can help you address your fears if this is something you struggle with.

6. Dissociation

According to Mental Health America (MHA), dissociation is a mental experience that causes a person to disconnect from their present circumstances, thoughts, memory and identity. Like most symptoms, dissociation exists on a spectrum from mild to severe. Dissociation is common in people who have lived through trauma.

7. Experiencing Internal Rage

Uncontrollable anger is one of the nine classic symptoms of BPD, and quiet borderlines are not immune to experiencing it. Though they may not act outwardly on their anger, the emotion itself can be intense and difficult to handle.

8. Fear of Abandonment

Making frantic efforts to avoid abandonment is one of the hallmark symptoms of BPD, and affects almost all people with the diagnosis. If fear of abandonment is impacting your day-to-day functioning and relationships, you might benefit from trying out "Wise Mind," a dialectical behaviour therapy (DBT) skill recommended for folks with BPD.

9. Self-Sabotage

Self-sabotage, or a deliberate attempt to interfere with one's growth or goals, can be common for folks with BPD — especially if they struggle with self-harm tendencies. If you can relate, you're not alone. To connect with people who understand, we encourage you to post on The Mighty with the hashtag #CheckInWithMe.

10. Feeling Suicidal or Wanting to Self-Harm After Social Interactions

One of the most notable parts of BPD is having unstable and stormy interpersonal relationships. When quiet borderlines experience social rejection or letdowns, they may have painful internal experiences like suicidal thoughts or engage in self-harm.

11. Shutting Down

In classic "quiet" style, a person with quiet BPD is more likely to internalize and shut down rather than act out or lash out.

Chapter 13:

Five Inspiration Pillars For Men

The Traditional Man

Much has been said (and written too) about the traditional man. But, who really is he? The traditional man is the same as the modern man except that he was what society viewed masculinity at the time.

Men were known to be ruthlessly fierce with zero emotions. Their hearts solely performed the blood circulation function, nothing more. Actually, nobody knew how it felt to be a man except for men themselves. They hardly ever talked about it, so the guesswork continued.

The modern man has inherited the software of his predecessor and he is programmed in the same way. The advent of women empowerment was initially opposed by male chauvinists but they later bowed down.Thisis the reason why the gospel of feminism is not new to the ears of every lady out there.

The Road To Manhood Is Muddy And Swampy

After the empowerment of the female gender (which they rightfully deserved after being 'ruled' by men), the modern man was not taught how to handle the empowered woman.

It has been a push and pull lifestyle – instead of a complementary one – and this has not been any easier for Adam's gender.

However, men are still men. Where do they get the inspiration to wake up daily and chase their dreams? In the UK, the BBC in 2019 reported that domestic violence abuse against men has been on the rise and many more men are suffering in silence.

Pillars of inspiration

Despite all the difficulties, for hard times make a man, five pillarsare of great inspiration to men. Here they are:

1. Physical Strength

Men are proud of their masculine energy. They even brag about it!Their swiftness and agility in response areunmatched. Yes, there are physically fit ladies and it is a good thing. Men, however, take pride in it more.

From an early age, boys are raised up to go out on the field and play with their peers. They are also called upon to help with manual tasks. This discipline instilled in them is a source of inspiration to keep living their best life because the world needs them.

2. Source Of Income

This debate has never been settled – men are the traditional providers in families. In this era, roles are quickly changing and we have ladies too heading companies or working in different capacities to also fend for their families.

However, the pride of a man is hiswork. Regardless of how meager or plentiful they earn; men find pride in working for a living. Nothing is satisfying for a man like going back home with a day's wages or a monthly salary every month end. It makes him feel 'in charge'.

Work inspires men to live each day at a time even when work conditions are unfavorable.

3. The Traditional Leadership Advantage

Even with a changing society, families still look up to fathers for leadership. This does not make mothers any inferior. They still complement their husbands in making family decisions and that is beautiful.

Men are inspired to be better today than they were yesterday. They are an inspiration to younger males and would not want to let them down. This motivates them in their lives that they are still useful for they are expected to provide leadership.

4. Family

Families are the reason why men get out of bed daily for work. Most men arebreadwinners in their families.

If not for themselves, men are inspired by their families. Their wives and children are the motivation they need to live each day at a time.

5. Fellow Tribe Of Men

Iron sharpens iron, so is a responsible man molded by another. Other successful men inspire men to work hard each day and be successful like them.

It is some kind of a brotherhood that a man cannot fail his brother. Thisinspiration makes them wield tough situations of life just to make it in the end.

Here is what they did not tell you: being a man is difficult and at the same time, the easiest thing if you have the right motivation.

Chapter 14:

Five Ways Of Dealing With A Health Crisis

Health Crises

The world has not yet seen enough of them. Health crises have lately become very common and governments worldwide have their hands full. There are standard health procedures for such occurrences and they have been found useful in recent days.

Books of history have records of health crises that affected many parts of the world. They are the Flu pandemic (1889-1890), the American Polio epidemic (1916), the Spanish flu (1918-1920), the Asian flu (1957-1958), H1N1 swine flu (2009-2010), the Ebola pandemic (2014-2016) and the Coronavirus pandemic that is ravaging many parts of the world. Thesemajor health crises have raised the world's awareness and response to any future occurrence. While hoping for the best, the world is prepared to handle any eventuality.

There are ways of dealing with health crises. Here are five major ones:

1. Confirm The Outbreak

Every country has a national research institute that is depended upon to undertake research in the country's interest. They are equipped with the necessary modern technology for research purposes. The united states have the Centre for Disease Control (CDC), Britain has the national institute for health research (NIHR), and China has the China national health development research center (CNHDRC).

Such agencies are responsible for authoritatively confirming the outbreak in the country. They also have the duty of furnishing the country with the right description for the pandemic. It is important to get it right in the first place.

The right information will stop panic from citizens because they will know what they are facing.

2. Quarantine The Most Affected Areas

Data from hospitals will give an indication of the most affected areas by a disease. After the national health research body has confirmed the nature of the outbreak, the transmissibility of the disease can be determined. If it is an airborne disease or a fast communicable disease, quarantine of the most affected areas is recommended.

Quarantining is not discrimination. It keeps the rest of the population safe from contracting the disease. Medical attention can also be focused on such areas.

The national medical research agency can advise against quarantine if the disease is not communicable. It will also advise on how to keep the rest of the population safe. It can enroll mass vaccination exercises (if vaccines against the disease are available).

All measures put in place will depend on the magnitude of the health crisis.

3. Public Sensitization

The public is a major stakeholder that should not be overlooked. All medication is destined for them. They have the right to access information by the relevant authorities.

The government has the duty of informing its people about the health crisis they are facing. This should be done in a manner that will not cause panic or alarm.

Friendly communication can be done through digital and print media in all languages spoken in that specific country. Everyone should be able to understand the information from the government.

Enough official information will not give room to the spread of rumors. Unofficial information ismisleading and can cause unnecessary panic. Moreover, citizens can invent ineffective means of prevention or take harmful concoctions they believe is medicine.

4. Treat The Sick

Any health crisis will claim casualties. People may die in large numbers if they are not treated on time. The public should be sensitized to take their sick to hospitals for treatment. This is possible when the government has won public trust.

Understandably, some families may not be able to afford medical bills. This should not lock them out from treatment. The government can settle its bills. Health is the priority at this time.

The focus of the world and the nation should be on healing the people.

5. Periodically Review The Progress Made

In a health crisis, it is important to review progress made. This will help the nation make necessary adjustments. It is also a chance to rectify any wrong.

Since probably not the whole world could be affected by one health crisis, other nations can offer aid to their affected partners.

Dealing with health crises is not an everyday affair. The lives of people are on the line and one wrong move could cause the deaths of many people. Everything must be carefully thought out before execution.

Chapter 15:

How To Deal with Loss (People)

Coping with the loss of a close friend or family member may be one of the hardest challenges that many of us face. When we lose a spouse, sibling or parent our grief can be particularly intense. Loss is understood as a natural part of life, but we can still be overcome by shock and confusion, leading to prolonged periods of sadness or depression. The sadness typically diminishes in intensity as time passes, but grieving is an important process in order to overcome these feelings and continue to embrace the time you had with your loved one. Everyone reacts differently to death and employs personal coping mechanisms for grief. Research shows that most people can recover from loss on their own through the passage of time if they have social support and healthy habits. It may take months or a year to come to terms with a loss. There is no "normal" time period for someone to grieve. Don't expect to pass through phases of grief either, as research suggests that most people do not go through stages as progressive steps.

If your relationship with the deceased was difficult, this will also add another dimension to the grieving process. It may take some time and thought before you are able to look back on the relationship and adjust to the loss.

Human beings are naturally resilient, considering most of us can endure loss and then continue on with our own lives. But some people may struggle with grief for longer periods of time and feel unable to carry out daily activities. Individuals with severe grief or complicated grief could benefit from the help of a psychologist or another licensed mental health professional with a specialization in grief.

Mourning the loss of a close friend or relative takes time, but research tells us that it can also be the catalyst for a renewed sense of meaning that offers purpose and direction to life.

Grieving individuals may find it helpful to use some of the following strategies to help them process and come to terms with loss:

- **Talk about the death of your loved one:**

  With friends or colleagues in order to help you understand what happened and remember your friend or family member. Avoidance can lead to isolation and will disrupt the healing process with your support systems.

- **Accept your feelings.**

You may experience a wide range of emotions from sadness, anger or even exhaustion. All of these feelings are normal and it's important to recognize when you are feeling this way. If you feel stuck or overwhelmed by these emotions, it may be helpful to talk with a licensed psychologist or other mental health professional who can help you cope with your feelings and find ways to get back on track.

- **Take care of yourself and your family**

Eating healthy foods, exercising and getting plenty of sleep can help your physical and emotional health. The grieving process can take a toll on one's body. Make sure you check in with your loved ones and that they are taking the necessary healthy steps to maintain their health.

- **Reach out and help others dealing with the loss**

Spending time with loved ones of the deceased can help everyone cope. Whether it's sharing stories or listening to your loved one's favourite music, these small efforts can make a big difference to some. Helping others has the added benefit of making you feel better as well.

- **Remember and celebrate the lives of your loved ones**

Anniversaries of a lost loved one can be a difficult time for friends and family, but it can also be a time for remembrance and honouring them. It may be that you decide to collect donations to a favourite charity of the deceased, passing on a family name to a baby or planting a garden in memory. What you choose is up to you, as long as it allows you to honour that unique relationship in a way that feels right to you.

Chapter 16:

How to achieve true forgiveness?

The qualification of forgiveness.

First things first, what is forgiveness? It is the process of accepting to let go of a grudge and forget the hurt that someone has done to you. We unintentionally hurt each other and sometimes ourselves. Your conscience pricks you when this happens and you want to create peace with either yourself or the other person. The question that stays in your mind all this while is whether or not what you have done qualifies for forgiveness. Yes, it does. Nothing is unforgivable.

Healthy relationships.

You need to have a healthy relationship with yourself before you can extend the same to other people. Forgiveness is an ingredient ofthe same. It shows that you prioritize your relationships over your hurt. It is selflessness at its peak. Let us demystify this fallacy —forgiveness is a licensefor other people to hurt you.On the contrary, it is not. It is an act of love that rises above any hurt done to you. There is no healthy relationship without forgiveness.

Dimensions of forgiveness

There are several perspectives of forgiveness. The first one is not being hard on yourself over a wrong you did. Sometimes you condemn yourself because you feel you could have done something yet you did not. This guilty conscience denies you peace until you embrace forgiveness. The second dimension is the impact of other people on you because you have not moved on from the hurt they caused. Both of these dimensionsimpact your performance directly. Strive for true forgiveness. This is the manual to forgiveness:

1. Identify the hurt.

The first step to forgiveness is identifying the hurt caused to you or other people. Blanket emotions can make you unable to pick exactly what caused the hurt. You cannot forgive yourself or someone for something unclear. Identifying the hurt is not to apportion blame on anyone for anything. It is getting the facts right about what indeed happened.

2. Confess your mistake.

This is the right way to ask for forgiveness,"I am sorry for hurting your feelings by saying those hurtful words yesterday night. I sincerely regret my actions and I am asking for your forgiveness." What strikes you in this apology? The reason for the apology is clear and it shows remorse. If you are the reason for hurting yourself, confess the same. This does not validate any hurt caused. Take the example of treatment at the hospital. You have to be diagnosed with the right illness before you are put on medication. This is what confession does.

3. Avoid the causes of hurt.

The next wisest step to complete the healing process is avoiding the causes of hurt altogether. A mistake repeated is a choice. Do not choose to hurt people knowingly. Learn from your previous mistakes. For example, think twice before speaking about the private lives of other people. This is a sensitive zone and you never know how deep it may hurt them. Being sensitive to their feelings and privacy is a way to honor your apology to them.

4. Build reconciliatory habits.

It is possible to turn a conflict into a blessing. You may have hurt someone unwillingly because you did not know it would offend them. An innocent casual talk could be the cause of a major fallout. True reconciliation does not end with seeking forgiveness. What follows isbuilding new reconciliatory habits that would prevent the re-occurrence of a conflict. For example, you are likely to insult someone else if you have a loose mouth. You would have reconciled with person A only to conflict with person B.It is better to build new habits to replace your bad old ones. Train yourself to bless people instead of cursing them and speaking your thoughts openly instead of gossiping behind their backs. The starting point is at identifying the hurt you caused and developing new habits to remedy it. A dry apology will not make up for the hurt you caused.

5. Open a new chapter.

Have you heard about this – forgive and forget? This is the hallmark of true forgiveness. Once you forgive someone, stop rubbing it on their face. Move on from there into new territories and explore them. Your previous experiences offered life lessons for you to carry to the new chapter. Do not let them hold you back.

Conclusion

You should embrace forgiveness as part of the healing process. True forgiveness will leave you whole again. It is a turning point for a better lifestyle.

Chapter 17:

Five Ways to Tell if an Introvert is Mad at You.

Who is an introvert and how do they express their feelings? These questions break the ice in the conversation aboutintroverts. An introvert is a person who feels more comfortable focusing on their inner thoughts rather than the outside world. They are not interested in crowds of people but engage selectively with a few people. Introverts are majorly in two forms. Some are naturally introverted and those who are so because of the prevailing circumstances. Despite their silence, introverts play an increasingly bigger role in a dynamic world. They can no longer be assumed. This is the reason why you have to go out of your way to understand their language (most of which is non-verbal). At face value, introverts appear to be emotionless and do not care about what happens when, and where. It will be misleading to assume this about introverts. They can be happy, sad, or angry like everybody else. Can you tell apart when they are in either of these moods? Here is how you can tell if an introvert is mad at you:

1. They want to be left alone.

Introverts indeed enjoy their own company. You should, however, be worried when they avoid your company and retreat to their 'safe zones.' It could be that you have pissed them off and do not want to see you. Normal people and extroverts will want to confront you for what you have done to them. It is their way of venting their grief. Introverts on the other hand want to go to a different world just to be away from you.

2. They refuse to answer your calls, texts, and emails.

A notable sign that an introvert is mad at you is that they will cut communication with you. They are not ready to have any conversation because you annoyed them. While some will still reply to your communication albeit slowly, others will give you the silent treatment and make it difficult for you to reach them. It is not safe to assume that an introvert is mad at you only because of the cut communication. There could be other reasons. Do not assume they are mad at you until you have proof.

3. They retreat to their work.

The workplace is where introverts feel safest. Most introverts bury themselves in work, not because they love working too much but because it is their escape route. In the introverts' dictionary, people can disappoint you but work does not. Work is where introverts hide after you have made them mad. It reassures them that they are still useful even when other people doubt them.

4. They refuse your help.

If you are the reason for hurting them, why would they still accept your offer for help? Of course, they will not. An introvert may not boldly tell you that they want nothing with you but their actions shall tell you the same. Extroverts may be willing to accept your help just in case you have changed. But it will take some time before you earn the trust of an introvert.

5. They respond with one-word answers.

"Yes" and "No" are some of the one-word answers introverts are fond of using. Although they hardly talk much, introverts will care to explain even a little when you engage them in a conversation. The one-word answers that introverts give are a sign that they want nothing to do with you. Check if you have brushed them the wrong way and seek reconciliation with them.

Being an introvert is one of the best personality traits yet very confusing for most people to understand. They are mostly men and women of their word. These five signs will help you know when they are mad at you.

Chapter 18:

8 Best Things To Do In Your Free Time

If you have a lot of free time, the best way to use it is to relax, have fun, de-stress after a stressful day, or spend time with a loved one. But if you only have a small portion - say 5 or 10 minutes - you don't have time for exciting stuff. So what do you do in your free time? Take these small chunks of time to make the most of them. Everyone works differently, so making the best use of your free time depends on you, your work style, and what's on your to-do list. But it's handy to have a list like this so you can quickly figure out how to spend that spare time working right away without thinking. Use the following checklist to get ideas for what you can do in the short term.

1. Reading Files

Clip articles from magazines, print out good articles or reports to read later, and keep them in a folder labelled "Reading File". Take it with you wherever you go, and whenever you have some spare time, you can remove items from your reading file. Keep a reading file on your computer (or in your bookmarks) for a quick read at your desk (or on the road if you have a laptop).

2. Clear Out Inbox

A meeting in 5 minutes? Use it to empty your physical or electronic inbox. If you have a lot of things in your inbox, you will have to work quickly, and you may not get everything done; but reducing your stack can be a big help. And having an empty inbox is a great feeling.

3. Phone Calls

Keep a list of the phone calls you need to make and the phone number, and take it with you wherever you go. Whether you're at your desk or on the go, you can remove a few calls from your list in no time

4. Make Money

It's my favourite effective use of free time. I have a list of articles to write, and when I have a few minutes to spare, I will write half a paper quickly. If you have 5-10 free time a day, you can earn a decent side income. Figure out how you can leverage your freelance skills and prepare work you can get done quickly - break it down into chunks, so the pieces can be done in time short.

5. File

No one likes to do that. If you're on your game, you'll sort things out at once, so they don't pile up on top of each other. But if you've just been through a hectic period, you probably have many documents or files lying around. Or maybe you have a large stack of papers to file. Cut that number down with every bit of spare time you have, and you'll be on the Nirvana leaderboards soon.

6. Reading

Reading is a lifelong skill, and successful people never stop reading new books. Whether fiction or nonfiction, books help you better understand your world. They introduce you to new characters, environments, cultures, philosophies, and ideas and can even help you learn new skills (at least if you read nonfiction). Likewise, reading regularly helps build your vocabulary and semantic understanding, giving you better communication skills and what to do for small talk during difficult business meetings. Handle that.

7. Volunteer

No matter how or where you do it, volunteering benefits you and your community. Whether you're helping clean up a highway, working at a soup kitchen or mentoring a group of young professionals, your time will help you improve the communities around you in the long run. Successful professionals recognize the importance of giving back to the community and feeling happier. Volunteering is also a valuable networking experience, introducing you to others who, in one way or another, can help you advance in your career.

8. Spend Time With Friends And Family

Your job is not everything. Focusing too much on your career is self-destructive, which seems counterintuitive. Suppose you want to be successful in life. In that case, you need to prioritize your relationships with friends and family members. No matter how quickly you want to succeed and climb the corporate ladder, you can't neglect your friends and family to do it.

Conclusion

If you don't spend your free time like this, that doesn't mean you don't have a chance of success. However, by adopting some of these strategies, you can extend your network to levels that improve your skills, thinking, and opportunities for success in the workplace. When you start incorporating some of these into your off-duty routines, you may be surprised at the results.

Chapter 19:

Six Ways To Stop Procrastinating

Why Procrastinate?

There are a million reasons why you should postpone what you intend to do. Procrastination can come in many ways, most of which are very attractive. Its repercussions are severe and unforgiving. You could miss out on once-in-a-lifetime opportunities and you will have no one to blame but yourself.

It's not a surprise that you may have unsuccessfully tried to stop procrastinating. Here are tried, tested, and proven six ways how you can overcome it:

1. Be Decisive

Your indecisiveness is the reason why you always postpone your scheduled activities. Purpose to be proactive. When you think about doing something, act immediately. Do not shelf any plans you may have for whatever reason no matter how genuine it may look. There is never an opportune time to act.

If you may require resources to implement your plan, move towards getting them instead of waiting for someone else. Try to be self-dependent instead of relying much on other people's help.

However, you will have to operate on other people's schedules if you always depend on them. Get things done yourself and help shall find you halfway.

2. Think Out Aloud

This is effective especially for very forgetful people. They procrastinate even in the few times they remember. An important lesson is that there is never a next time.

Instead of making mental notes about what you plan to do, say it aloud. You are likely to remember what you said aloud more than what was in your mind. Keep reminding yourself by saying aloud (not too loud) what you want to do shortly.

This is helpful especially if you are alone. Constantly repeating the same thing can be a nuisance to the people you are with. Here is another way if you are not alone.

3. Enlist Your Friends' Help

If your plans are neither sensitive nor personal, you can ask the next person to remind you. Your involvement with other people will have them put you in check.

They will act as prefects over you. Since procrastination is a choice to postpone an act, having a second person who knows what you are supposed to do will enforce personal accountability. You are more likely to ignore what you enlisted to do alone than when someone else is 'monitoring' you.

4. Fix Yourself First

You could be blaming your procrastination on other things when you are the problem. You can hardly see the problem within yourself. As much as there could be other causes of procrastination, do a self-audit of yourself.

Are you lacking the psyche to do anything? If you literally need to be pushed even if there is an urgency for you to act, then you are the problem.

Read motivational literature on personal development to lift your spirit. You can also talk to people who will inspire you to action. Motivated people do not procrastinate.

5. Fix Your Attitude Towards Work

Regardless of the level of your motivation, you will procrastinate if you have a bad attitude towards work. Check on your attitude towards what you often procrastinate about.

Do you love what you do or you would rather be doing something else? Have a good attitude towards everything you do and you will have the motivation to do what it is.

You can know your attitude through your thoughts. If you have bad thoughts about an act, you will always procrastinate when it comes to implementing it. A good attitude will make you swift in your action.

6. Plan Ahead

While the problem could not be about lacking a good plan, it is important to check on your plans if you want to stop procrastination.

Group similar activities together and implement them to completion before starting other tasks. It is easier to complete tasks when you cluster them together based on their characteristics.

For example, labor-intensive work should be done together. Mental tasks should be grouped to be done together too.

These six ways will help you be prompt in your actions and stop procrastination.

Chapter 20:

Stop Overthinking

Thinking optimally.

Thinking is healthy for everybody. The fact that you do not think about anything is a red flag. Thinking gives you a range of choices in decision-making. You can evaluate one after another before settling for the best. Good thinking is not a choice we have anyway. If you do not do it, somebody else will exploit you by thinking on your behalf. They may not act in good faith and you will be the victim.

Thinking is healthy and normal for any sane person. However, there are upper and lower limits in thinking. Retarded thinking will disable you from living or working optimally. Similarly, overthinking will deny you serenity in life.

Threshold of thoughts to entertain.

We should not every thoughtregardless of how enticing they are because their effects could be disastrous. We should sieve whatever we give attention to whileallowing only the best to occupy our minds. However, do we have control over our thoughts?

Most people cannot take charge of their thoughts because they have not set their priorities right. Their minds cannot prioritize what is important because of their indecisiveness. They cannot let go of an idea or situation once they start pondering on it.

Overthinking is highly unrecompensed. Here are a few ways on how to stop it:

- **Accept fate**

Fate is unchallengeable. There is a different way to handle it if it is unfavorable. Living in denial will complicate matters instead of making them better. Be optimistic when doors shut in front of you. Consider it a way nature is warning you about the path you have chosen.

The universe naturally selects the best for us. Its blessings could come in unexpected ways. When we misjudge them for misfortunes, we will spend much time overthinking what we should have thanked the universe for.

Accepting fate is not giving up. It is stopping to overthink non-issues and moving on to more important ones. Overthinking is injurious to an uncertain future. We can bulldoze our way in things that we could have just left alone. Such mistakes are expensive to commit.

- **Count your blessings.**

One reason why people overthink is the fear of losing. It clouds their judgment to the extent of not remembering their past achievements. Think enough to get past a hurdle but do not prolong it further. Overthinking will not make problems go away. Instead, it could complicate them more.

Whenever you find yourself overthinking about something, retract your steps and be grateful for your achievements. Gratitude will open your eyes to the reality that you did not make it because of overthinking. Other factors were part of your success.

Overthinking will blind you from acknowledging your past victories. Fight it by reminding yourself that it had nothing to do with your success.

- **Prioritize your health.**

A healthy lifestyle is worry-free. You can stop overthinking when you consider the status of your health. It does more harm than good. People with underlying health conditions like high blood pressure and diabetes are advised by doctors not to overthink for the sake of their health.

Overthinking could trigger ulcers. For the sake of good health, strive not to overthink trivial issues. Whenever you start overthinking, remember what it can do to your health. Prioritize your health above everything.

Consider the analogy of cigarette smokers and the health warning written boldly on the packets. If they could take the warning seriously, a majority of them would not fall to lung-related complications in old age. Similarly, there is a warning to stop overthinking in life lest you succumb to depression and anxiety.

In conclusion, it is paramount to stop overthinking because it changes nothing. Its demerits outweigh its benefits. It is a passive way of dealing with challenges. Instead of worrying about a problem, be proactive in seeking solutions.

When the burden of overthinking gets heavy, share it with your friends and you will find a solution together.

Chapter 21:

Ten Life Principles To Follow

Trust The Process

It is not the first time that you are told to trust the process. What is hardly said is the details of the process. Nobody cares to share.

This process is conceived in your mind first. You have to be determined to follow it to the latter. It has no shortcuts but is worth the struggle.Consider it as a path chosen for you by destiny and it shall make you the great person you desire to be.

Well, here is a 10 step process that you can trust entirely with your life.

Step 1: Self-Awareness

Self-awareness is key in your transformation to be the next hero. What do you identify yourself with? What you associate yourself with is very importantregardless of your background. Let nothing pin you down.

Becoming self-aware is knowing your worth and fighting for it. The higher your value, the higher your prize.

Step 2: Progress over Success

Success is an amorphous term. Do not beat yourself over it. It is not easy to define it because it means different things to different people.

Instead of pursuing success, seek progress. It is visible and can be measured. Progress can be evaluated and be appraised. In pursuing progress, you will find success.

Step 3: Be Visionar

Vision goes beyond sight. It is what you can see with your eyes still closed. Develop a vision for yourself. This is something that will pursue your entire life. It is your mission statement.

A good vision will make you progressive. It creates timelines for the attainment of your goals. When it goes dark, your vision will help you stay on course. You will not lose focus on the path you have chosen.

Step 4: Choosing Vision Bearers Wisely

Vision bearers conceive your vision. They are there to support your journey through life. They will counsel and support you throughout; never leaving your side.

Be careful in choosing such partners. They can make your vision stall without you knowing it. Trusting this team with your vision could be your best or worst decision ever.

Step 5: Be Decisive

Decisiveness is being firm in your choices. Your affirmative should remain so and your negative should be firm. You should be convinced by only facts.

Being decisive will make you a good decision-maker. Such sound decisions are good for the realization of your vision.

Step 6: Handling Enemies

It is inevitable to make enemies as you progress in life. Some people may not wish you well for selfish reasons. If you do not take care, they can pull you down very fast.

Be swift in identifying enemies and cut them off your circle. Be ruthless and decisive with them. If they tried to harm you once, they will do it again when they have the chance.

Step 7: Handling Personal Struggles

There are some personal battles that we must wage ourselves. It is prudent not to assign somebody else duties that require your personal attention.

Choosing your life partner is one task that you should not delegate. One wrong move could undo the empire you have tried to build your whole life.

Step 8: Face Your Fears

Running from your fears will not help solve anything. It gives you a sense of a false win. Confront your fears head-on.

What frightens you can possibly chase you from your empire. Once you learn to fight them, your rule shall be established.

Step 9: Fight Pride

Pride can sneak on you silently and before you know it, you are on your way down from the top. It is an imminent threat to your success.

Do not entertain a lot of praises from people. They may get into your head and make you carefree. Respond modestly to praise.

Step 10: Find Comfort In Solitude

Do not be too much fond of the company of other people. You are more likely to be corrupted. They will also get used to you and your value in them will diminish.

Enjoy your own company. Go for those walks alone to clear your mind. Reason prevails in solitude.

This is the 10 step manual to achieving greatness.

Chapter 22:

Ten psychological lessons not taught in school.

The value of psychology

Psychology lessons are very important. There's a bit of it that is taught in schools but a huge chunk is not. The four walls of a classroom cannot accommodate all life psychological lessons. This does not undervalue the input of schools in education. They are equally important in raising responsible adults. You have to learn both classroom and life lessons to be an all-aroundperson. Here is a spotlight on ten psychological lessons not taught in school:

1. Emotions are destructive.

Unbridled emotions are like a ticking time bomb. It will one day explode when you least expect it. Always learn to handle your emotions before they get out of hand. It does not matter how justifiable they are. They are a liability if they cannot beput in check. Schools teach the superficial importance of managing your emotions. You are not told how quickly good emotions can flip to be dangerous.Never make any decision at the peak of emotions. Decision-making requires sobriety.

2. Do not be controlled by rage.

No matter how hard you try, you are not immune to anger. Sometimes your patience is pushed to the limits and you can feel the world crumble at your fingertips. Never act out of anger because revenge will blind you not to act objectively. Once you are out of school, you will realize that you can be prosecuted if you harm someone with your rage. Anger is not immune from the law. Learn to manage it early enough before it fails you later.

3. Stand out.

Always maintain a good work ethic whether or not you are being supervised. This will build your character and make you beyond reproach. Let the quality of your work testify about your character. This will build your network and help you create more meaningful connections. Do not allow yourself to blend in the background. Other people should not absorb you. Stand out as the leader wherever you go. This is a bonus to your reputation.

4. Actions over arguments.

How do you react to confrontation? Do not be quick to engage in a war of words. Instead, prove your opponents wrong through your actions. They speak louder than words, right? Arguments make you appear weak incapable of proving his point without throwing tantrums. You would not want this tag, would you?

5. Mind your words.

Weigh your words carefully before you speak. People may forget what happened but never forget how you made them feel. Do not underestimate the power of the tongue. Your words can win someone over or send them away. Speaking too much makes you prone to mistakes. You may lose the trust of those who respected you when you err in speech.

6. Build confidence.

Have enough self-confidence to believe in yourself before other people believe in you. Trust in your vision and ability to handle things maturely. Do not second guess anything. Cultivate a good relationship with yourself and others. Love yourself for who you are and do not consider changing into another person. Let people fall in love with your personality and not what you are offering.

7. People are selfish.

Remember this before you enlist anybody's help. They will only be willing to help you out if it benefits them in some way. Not everyone is willing to help without a secret agenda. Always have something rolled up your sleeves for them. Make them believe that it will also benefit them in a way. Even so, do not be amazed when they turn on you and pursue their interests.

8. Stay fortified.

You should never let your guard down even when you think it is safe. You never know when the enemy will strike. It does not mean that you should always be paranoid. You have to be on the lookout justin case. Develop your strengths and consolidate your abilities. If possible, have a specialization. Be an expert at something instead of being a jack of all trades.

9. The calm rush.

This principle is about proper time management. Time is a very useful resource that cannot be recovered when wasted. Know exactly when to strike and when to retreat. Most people fail at this stage. Your time in school was controlled by bells. There is no such thing in the outside world. Wrong timing is an expensive mistake.

10. Calculated value.

Do not be comfortable in freebies. Nothing is free. There is always a price for it, even when it is not monetary. Learn to buy things yourself instead of relying on handouts. It lowers your standards and strips you of your dignity.

Conclusion

The list of psychology lessons in life is endless. Be a good student of life and keep learning.

Chapter 23:

Ten ways to become mentally stronger.

Mental strength is a very great asset. Seek to grow it daily and you shall stand out from the crowd. There is one true test of knowing your mental strength. Seek to know the honest opinion of people whom you have interacted with. They can assess you better on how you responded to issues that required your attention. The good news is that there are tried, tested, and proven ways on how you can increase your mental strength. Here are ten ways:

1. Having healthy debates.

Debates form an important part of growing your mental strength and social skills. There are two sides to every debate. Persuading your opponents that your position of the matter being discussed is the right way and not theirs is an uphill task. You cannot shout them down to submission or physically pull them over to your side. Listen to good debaters' debates and watch how they ask very important questions. Your mental strength grows as you engage like-minded people in critical thinking. It takes one sharp mind to strengthen another because iron sharpens iron.

2. Taking interest in mathematics and science.

All subjects are equally important. Mathematics and science just engage the mind a little bit more than others. These subjects involve a lot of logic and accurate analysis which is why they are fit to strengthen your mind.Start reading scientific theories that explain the difficult phenomenon. This will make you question what you considered normal. You will become mentally stronger with every analysis you make.

3. Learn to accept defeat.

A mentally strong person knows that defeat is an important part of learning. It means you have not got it right but learned another way of how not to do things. Defeat will not break you down when you accept it as part of life. You emerge stronger every time people expect you to succumb to it.

4. Believe in philosophy or religion.

Philosophy and religion hold very important pillars for society. They seek to explain what is a mystery to date. The creation and evolution stories are examples of theories developed to explain the origin of man.When you follow either of them, you will ask hard questions about particular beliefs that most people hold to date. This is your path to freedom of your mind!

5. Play mind games.

Do you know that all work without play makes Jack a dull boy? An important part of the play is mind games. They include reverse psychology intending to get other people to reveal their true intentions. Mind games help build a strong mind because you can penetrate the mind of another person through a simple conversation. You study their responses and attitude to life and you can choose whether or not to keep them as friends.

6. Improving your concentration.

How long and how deep you can concentrate on a single subject is very important. You should be capable of doing that for a longer period than the average person if you want to be mentally stronger. Do not give in to distractions when you are focusing on something. Think about its breadth and depth. Consider all the variables present and you will be able to make the right choice.

7. Understanding over cramming.

Many people will choose to cram over understanding because it is the shorter route. Yes, it could be shorter but it reduces your mental strength. A mentally stronger person can explain a new concept in their words as they understood it. Students who understand their teachers instead of cramming what they are taught are mentally strong. Make an effort to understand new things even if it is in small parts. The mind can never be full. You can only be tired but you can resume from where you paused it.

8. Keep the company of mentally gifted people.

Other people are mentally gifted. They understand new concepts the moment they are taught. Their analysis of everything is excellent and you can hardly find a fault with their thinking patterns. When you hang out with them, you will be able to study their thinking and approach. You can borrow a few skills from their prowess. Knowledge, like foolishness, is contagious. Beware of your company.

9. Embrace challenges.

Mental strength can increase or decrease. It is dependent on one major factor – challenges. Do not run away from challenges. Face them head-on. The same challenge will not come to you twice and it will leave you better than how it found you. This does not mean you should go looking for trouble. Only handle whatever comes your way. Have an open mind that the challenge you are facing is a lesson in preparation for your next step in life.

10. Meet new people.

Making new friends is not entirely a bad idea. Strangers can turn out to be best friends and even family! Your mind should be exposed to how different people run their things and their different approaches towards life. New people offer new experiences. These will strengthen your mind and approach to diversity.

Conclusion

The mind is like a muscle. Do not be afraid of committing mistakes. They offer a correction point of getting it right the next time. Practicing these ten ways will leave you mentally stronger.

Chapter 24:

Ten Ways To Make This Your Best Year

Not Business As Usual

"Happy new year!" This was on everyone's lips at the beginning of the year. We wished each other well and we were full of expectations about what this year will bring to our tables.

What is so unique in this year that was missing in the previous one? Only one thing. Your age. It is the only thing that is in constant motion. Having new year resolutions helps a lot. If you did not achieve your last year's, this too shall be unachieved. You can take that to the bank. You have to change your tactic if you want to make this your best year ever. Here are ten ways you can achieve this:

1. Set Realistic Goals

You know your limits and what you are capable of. Your target should lie within those ranges. Do not overstretch yourself beyond your limits. You may not achieve much.

It is okay to have high dreams but take one step at a time if you want to maximize your potential. Unrealistic goals will instill worry in you and in this state, you really cannot do much.

2. Rest But Do Not Quit

It is not okay toquit on the ambitions you have for this new year.
Resting to rejuvenate your strength and you will recover from any setback you have suffered. This new year shall be your best ever if you learn to rest.

3. Consider A Self-Care Routine

Self-care is a very important routine. It will make you celebrate yourself more and be proud of who you are.
You need to be in the best form ever as you pursue your goals. Cheer yourself on and fall in love more with yourself this year.

4. Benchmark With Successful People

Successful people have a wealth of experience in whatever it is they do. First, identify what spikes your interest and the people successful in that field.
Learn from them what makes themstand out and implement the same in your projects. You will definitely have the same results as them.

5. Spend Time With Your Family

Family is the basic and most valuable unit a person can have. Despite all your busy schedules, spare some time for your family. They are the backbone of your success.

The more you spend time with people who value you, the more you also get to appreciate yourself. Do not waste any opportunity to unite with your family.

6. Follow Your Passion

Follow your passion at all costs for therein lies your success. If you have a passion for something, you invest your energy and resources in it. You also become more knowledgeableabout it.

Do not follow other people for the sake of it. Be unique in your own way and you shall be rewarded for it.

7. Do Not Procrastinate

When you settle on doing something, do not postpone its actualization. Better yet, when a worthy idea comes into your mind, write it down in a notebook before you forget.

Thereafter, plan on how you can implement the idea. There is stiff competition in every industry. While you postpone your idea, another person elsewhere will implement it.

8. Consult Widely

Accept that you do not have a monopoly on ideas. Consult with more experienced people than you. They will advise you accordingly on how you can go about new ideas.

Wide consultation will give you the perspective of many people. You can thereafter sieve through the advice you have been given and act on the best one.

9. Go For Health Check-Ups Periodically

Health is wealth. You should pay attention to your health. Do not wait to go to the hospital at the last minute. Routine health check-ups are good because some diseases can be diagnosed on time and you can get treatment.

Of what use is all the wealth you will accumulate if will not be healthy to enjoy it?

10. Set Up A Workout Routine

A workout routine is important for a healthy lifestyle. Enroll for gym sessions nearby and start working out today. It is not always about burning calories but staying fit and healthy.

Exercises will also improve your mental health. You will be stress-free as you follow up on your goals.

Start a new beginning today to make this your best year.

Chapter 25:

The Psychology of Money

Psychology is the scientific study of the human mind and human behaviour. The field also includes the study of conscious and unconscious phenomena, including feelings and thoughts. The strides made in this field have transformed the way humans think and behave, and this also extends into the field of investments. Investors are human beings before anything else, after all.

Breakthroughs in psychology have made public phenomena collectively known as biases. Psychological biases are errors in thinking that are often influenced by faulty reasoning and emotions or feelings. These biases affect the way capital market players make decisions regarding investments and, in turn, returns. An awareness of these biases can help investors better understand themselves so that they make better investment decisions.

Loss Aversion

This is a tendency to experience more disutility for a loss compared to the utility experiences for a similar magnitude in a gain. In other words, the loss in happiness over a $2 loss is often larger than the happiness one experiences when they make a $2 gain. In capital markets, this bias manifests in premature profit-taking when the market rallies and holding onto loss-making positions for a much longer period than necessary. Investors exhibiting loss aversion often leave money on the table by selling stocks with strong positive momentum early in the bull run, and they incur more losses because they hold onto loss-making positions for longer periods of time. On the ZSE, the relatively higher turnover during a bull run compared to a bear run partly hints to the existence of loss aversion among investors on the bourse. One way to circumvent this bias is to adopt a research-driven framework that will allow investors to take full advantage of price rallies by maintaining their equity position until the stock(s) in question exceed their respective target price and cutting losses by responding swiftly to new and material information that changes the case for a loss-making equity position.

Mental Accounting

This is a tendency to mentally group money in different "accounts" based on how it was earned and the goals that each account needs to achieve. An investor could have separate funds invested for each goal that they have, and these investments are constructed separately. However, these mental accounts are often poorly structured from a holistic point of view, and the overall portfolio is poorly diversified and sub-optimal. A prudent approach to a goals-driven investment strategy that addresses mental accounting is to construct a portfolio that acknowledges the fungibility of money, that is, money is all the same regardless of how it is earned or the goal it is intended to achieve. One could treat money received from a refund, rebate or an arbitrage trade as "free money" and use it on discretionary goods instead of considering it as funds that can be used to achieve other goals, such as investing for retirement or clearing debt.

Availability

This bias stems from taking mental shortcuts to information processing. This "rule of thumb" thinking often results in information processing being influenced by information that the brain easily retrieves, a narrow range of experiences, familiar categorisations, etc. This bias often leads to a rise in overly risk-averse investors after a recession or a market crash. Similarly, bull runs often result in an increase in overly aggressive investors taking long positions at the tail end of a stock's momentum. In some instances, investors make decisions by drawing parallels from their own experiences, like avoiding investing in a stock because they made a big loss the last time that they took positions in the same stock. Investors must make decisions with guidance from fundamental and technical indicators that appropriately quantify recent information if they wish to avoid the availability bias.

Status quo

This bias is often synonymous with the "if it ain't broke, don't fix it" mentality, where people choose to do nothing rather than make a change because of no apparent problem in sight. However, this bias can lead to problems in the case of an investor holding a volatile and illiquid equity portfolio when the market experiences a downturn, for example. An awareness of the risk-reducing and return-enhancing benefits of asset diversification and efficient asset allocation can drive investors to make market-influenced changes to their portfolios regularly.

There are over 190 psychological biases that have been documented and the onus remains on investors to explore these and see how they affect their investment decision-making process. A comprehensive cognitive bias codex can be found on *Wikipedia* and many other sources of information available online.

Chapter 26:

Mindfulness Over Anxiety

Anxiety The Thief!

You may not realize it until the moment it steals your joy. Anxiety is the modern-day thief that deprives people of their joy. It camouflages behind various excuses but finally reveals its true colors. It is just a matter of time.

Anxiety instills worry for no good reason. All of a sudden you start to think 'what if things go wrong' when nothing has happened yet. This mentality will lie that you are planning aheadwhile the reality is that you are overstretching your ability. There is only so much that you can control.

Cheat Anxiety Today!

When you are anxious about something, your body will naturally respond to your fears. You tend to breathe a little faster than the normal rate, some people will sweat in their palms, and you will be absent-minded. Your mind will wander to how you can rescue yourself from the fix you find yourself in.

You can overcome anxiety in two ways: the short way and the longdurable one.

The shorter way is regulating your basal metabolic rate. Here is what you should do whenever you are anxious. Inhale and exhale slowly paying attention to only the flow of air into and out of your lungs. Close your eyes as you do this.

Repeating this procedure will calm you down, your breathing rate will return to normal and you will regain your composure in a while.

While you may have beaten anxiety at the moment, you need a durable solution for it.

Mindfulness It Is!

Mindfulness is prioritizing logic over emotions no matter how strong they may be. Whenever you are anxious, tell yourself "mindfulness over anxiety."

It happens in several ways but here are proven ways to overcome anxiety:

1. Take Caution

Most people throw caution to the wind about other matters except their cause for anxiety.

This is a dangerous trend because instead of curing anxiety, it will shift it elsewhere. Solving one problem only to create another is a cycle you will not want to be in.

Since anxiety is caused by worry, when you are careful about what you do there will be no cause for worry because you will ensure what is in your control unfolds just fine. Tie any loose ends to your plans to reduce risk and you will not have to worry about mishaps.

2. Build Healthy Relationships

You are probably anxious about somebody else's reaction because the both of you have not bonded well. This gives room to insecurities – a very unhealthy component of relationships.

It is difficult to be anxious about people that do not matter. The people you love and care for the most are the ones responsible for your anxiety. Endeavor to build healthy relationships with them so that you can be confident of expressing yourself to them on anything, whether good or bad.

Healthy relationships are our refuge even during anxious moments and they should not be the very cause of our trouble.

3. Nourishing Your Mind

You should constantly feed your mind with the right things. Failure to do this, our fears take root and it becomes difficult to remove them.

Read widely and fill your mind with knowledge. Expand your expertise in science, astronomy, and whatever interests you. This will give no room for fear and anxiety to thrive.

Moreover, you can come up with solutions to what causes anxiety if you have the right skills. We are anxious when we are helpless. Having the knowledge to 'rescue' ourselves from such moments is good because we will always be in charge.

4. Planning To Reduce Risk

Uncertainty is what causes anxiety. The future is a gamble and not everything is guaranteed. When you plan, you will feel more secure and so will the people you are with. There will be surety about many things that would have otherwise cost you sleepless nights.

Mindfulness over anxiety includes these four and many other steps to curb anxiety before it even sprouts. You shall eventually emerge victoriously.

Chapter 27:

How Volunteering Can Make You Happy

With busy lives, it can be hard to find time to volunteer. However, the benefits of volunteering can be enormous. Volunteering offers vital help to people in need, worthwhile causes, and the community, but the benefits can be even greater for you, the volunteer. The right match can help you to find friends, connect with the community, learn new skills, and even advance your career.

Giving to others can also help protect your mental and physical health. It can reduce stress, combat depression, keep you mentally stimulated, and provide a sense of purpose. While it's true that the more you volunteer, the more benefits you'll experience, volunteering doesn't have to involve a long-term commitment or take a huge amount of time out of your busy day. Giving in even simple ways can help those in need and improve your health and happiness.

One of the more well-known benefits of volunteering is the impact on the community. Volunteering allows you to connect to your community and make it a better place. Even helping out with the smallest tasks can make a real difference to the lives of people, animals, and organizations in need. And volunteering is a two-way street: It can benefit you and your family as much as the cause you choose to help. Dedicating your time as a volunteer helps you make new friends, expand your network, and boost your social skills.

One of the best ways to make new friends and strengthen existing relationships is to commit to a shared activity together. Volunteering is a great way to meet new people, especially if you are new to an area. It strengthens your ties to the community and broadens your support network, exposing you to people with common interests, neighbourhood resources, and fun and fulfilling activities.

While some people are naturally outgoing, others are shy and have a hard time meeting new people. Volunteering gives you the opportunity to practice and develop your social skills, since you are meeting regularly with a group of people with common interests. Once you have momentum, it's easier to branch out and make more friends and contacts.

Volunteering helps counteract the effects of stress, anger, and anxiety

The social contact aspect of helping and working with others can have a profound effect on your overall psychological well-being. Nothing relieves stress better than a meaningful connection to another person. Working with pets and other animals has also been shown to improve mood and reduce stress and anxiety.

Volunteering combats depression

Volunteering keeps you in regular contact with others and helps you develop a solid support system, which in turn protects you against depression.

Volunteering makes you happy

By measuring hormones and brain activity, researchers have discovered that being helpful to others delivers immense pleasure. Human beings are hard-wired to give to others. The more we give, the happier we feel.

Chapter 28:

How To Stop Worrying and Go To Sleep

Have trouble falling asleep, staying asleep or just feeling rested? The bad news is that it may be due to personal lifestyle habits. However, the good news is that those are easy to change to help get you on your way to sleeping better.Some people lay in bed staring at the ceiling in part due to chronic pain, depression, medications or other substances that can interfere with sleep. When you treat those issues, often it will naturally help improve your ability to sleep.

However, despite addressing other medical or psychiatric conditions, sleep difficulties often will persist. People who have chronic insomnia worry excessively about sleep and the effects of insomnia. They also become more and more agitated and tense as bedtime gets closer.If you're very worried about getting good sleep, you can put a lot of effort into getting sleep and have a lot of anxiety at night. This makes you more alert and can keep you lying in bed wide awake.

We are offering some suggestions that can help improve your sleep habits, including individuals who suffer from chronic insomnia. Trying to break some of the patterns that you may have developed is often the key.

Keep your sleep schedule the same

You can improve your sleep by ensuring that you have a consistent sleep schedule. Avoid staying up late on weekends and sleeping in, then trying to go to bed at your regular time on Sunday night. We call it social jet lag because it's like you've flown to California, and now you're trying to adjust back to the time zone difference. So, keep those times as consistent as you can."Going to bed early or sleeping in to catch up only leads to more fragmented and poor quality sleep. Typically, you go to bed two hours early and then just lay there wide awake, continuing to associate your bed with not sleeping.

Take some quiet time before bedtime

Quiet time is worth its weight in gold. Give yourself at least 30 to 60 minutes of quiet, relaxed time before bed as a buffer. Nix phone screen time and replace it with reading a book, listening to calming music, taking a warm bath or having some decaffeinated herbal tea.

Distract yourself if you can't sleep

If you can't fall asleep, get up and try to restart by doing something to distract yourself before going back to bed. It could be flipping through magazines, calming yoga stretches or some type of relaxing hobby like knitting or colouring. Avoid anything that's goal-directed or too physically or mentally activating such as house chores, paying bills or working on a computer. While it may be tempting to grab your phone off your nightstand and scroll endlessly through social media, don't. The blue light emitted from your phone or tablet screen can inhibit your natural melatonin production which is a hormone that is involved in the timing of our internal circadian sleep clock.

Learn how to relax

Learning relaxation techniques such as meditation, guided imagery and progressive muscle relaxation can go a long way in helping you fall asleep. A sleep specialist can help you learn this as well as ways to calm your mind and your muscles and reduce or eliminate all the racing thoughts and worries. Dealing with stress in a healthy way is important for not only sleep, but your overall health, too."Practice the relaxation techniques and develop them as a skill during the day when you feel good and are already calm, rather than trying to do them for the first time at bedtime,"

Keep a sleep log

Think of this as the adult sister to that diary you've kept in middle school. You can track the details of your sleep patterns and lifestyle habits. This can help you see trends in your behaviour and will be useful when you discuss your insomnia with your doctor or a sleep disorder specialist. If writing things down the old fashioned way isn't your jam, try smartphone apps or your smartwatch to help you keep a log.

Chapter 29:

How to Persuade People Effortlessly

Have you ever met a person who ought to get you to do anything? I have, and I've continually craved this reputedly out-of-attain ability.

There are endless books and university publications that each one declares to preserve the keys to persuasion. They're treasured assets for getting to know a way to persuade; however, they generally tend to overcomplicate the problem and forget about sensible strategies of speaking efficiently with people.

You don't need to be a grasp salesman with limitless self-assurance with a purpose to be extra persuasive. You, without a doubt, want to pay nearer interest to the fundamentals so you can twist the chances of fulfillment in your favor.

1. Make Your Words Powerful

The pitch itself wishes to be complete of phrases that elicit a response. You can try this effortlessly by framing your statements around key phrases.

For example, "vehicle accident" is a word that makes you suspect many unique kinds of car collisions. But if you're attempting to steer a person to shop for vehicle insurance, you won't say that there are hundreds of vehicle injuries every day. You'll say that there are hundreds of vehicle-associated deaths each day.

"Death" is a greater effective phrase than "accident," and advertisers use this technique each day as a good way to persuade humans to shop for products.

2. Dress Up But Don't Look Down

Beautiful clothes will help you maintain your confidence even when no one is watching you. An unfortunate side effect is that being the most dressed person in the room can make you talk or humble yourself to taller people.

You are prone to this trap. When we feel empowered in a conversation, "Oh, then, let me explain this. It's really, really simple." The problem is that if it's not easy or if you don't communicate well, you're effectively lost.

Notice that the person you are talking to is taller than you. They have the right to refuse. You don't want them to realize this because you have to control the conversation, but talking to someone is challenging a contest you don't want to participate in. Remember, this is a penalty. The border between arrogance and dogmatism.

3. Focus On The Future

Using the future tense is a great way to build trust. It lets the other person know that you're moving forward and that you're ready to deliver on your promise.
You can do this easily by abusing the word will. Phrases like "We will" and "Then we will do this" will get the person used to the idea that this will happen.
That said, don't push yourself. Try not to make decisions for the other person, but instead talk about the possibilities and implications of the decisions that can be made.

4. Make Yourself Scarce

People want what they can't have. Make it clear that this offer you give them won't last forever and they'll miss it.
This is especially effective if you are selling a product. Common tactics for discounting new products are to intentionally make them scarce and unpopular, making people feel "Buy now while you can!"

5. Choose The Right Medium For Your Pitch

You're trying to convince someone to do something they probably don't (yet) want to do. This means it's essential to hone your pitch environment.

Research the person and determine how they want to communicate. Just ask them if they'd rather talk on the phone than email, as long as you give them a few options.

I've even met people who are more comfortable texting than talking face to face. Keep that in mind and choose media that focuses on them, not you.

6. Be A Master Of Timing

This goes hand in hand with knowing who you are proposing to. Research them and find out the best time to talk to them. For example, some very busy executives get overwhelmed at the start of the week and leave on Friday. This means Thursday could be the best time to approach someone you need to convince.

It will be easier to convince a friend or relative because you understand them better. Choose the right time to talk to them, and your chances of success will increase.

Remember that persuasion is a skill that can be honed and improved over time. You won't succeed the first time you practice these strategies (most likely), but the more often you use them, the more skilled and natural you will become at implementing them.

Be careful not to manipulate or intimidate people; your goal should instead help them see things differently.

Chapter 30:

Five things that destroy the first impression immediately

Death at first touch

We mostly know of love at first sight. The kind of love that rises like a tidal wave in the ocean to drown anyone and anything swimming in its vicinity. Love at first sight is powerful in its own right. It is instantaneous and strong. Nothing can stand before it if it is not made of love. However, there is also death at first touch. As the name goes, this kind of death finishes even the immortal love at first sight. Unlike love at first sight which is instantaneous, death at first touch takes time before it gets poisonous enough to kill the first-time impression. There is an amber alert before death itself comes to finish off the good first impression that you had spent time building.

Killers of the first impression

1. Bad attitude

Consider driving somewhere on a flat tire. Will you reach your destination on time? Of course not. You must have heard that a bad attitude is like a flat tire. If you do not change it, you won't go anywhere. You may have invested a lot in making a good first impression but death takes the form of a bad attitude and reverses all the favor that you had gained. Be careful how you relate publicly because people can lower you from the high pedestal they had put you all on account of your bad attitude. Develop a good attitude at all times and not only when it is convenient for you. People will be maintained by it even after meeting them for the first time. The reality of meeting someone with the best attitude ever is a big win in maintaining the first impression.

2. Impatience.

Patience or the lack of it is not written on the forehead. It is something that you only discover in someone after spending some time with them. You can manage to create an angel-like first impression on someone the first time you meet them. However, like anything good, this impression needs to be sustained. It can die a natural death when the other person discovers how impatient you are. Impatience makes you a lesser person by revealing your desperation to have things done at any cost. Guard the first impression people have on you by not complaining publicly. It can sometimes be mistaken for impatience yet you could avoid all this by holding your peace.

3. Pride.

They say that it comes before a fall. Nothing could be further from the truth. It is difficult to know whether or not someone is proud the first time you meet them. It is possible for them to carefully cover their tracks and present themselves as angelic beings. However, the moment you discover the pride in somebody you highly regarded, everything you felt for them immediately vaporizes. Pride is not a cloth that you put on or take off at your convenience. It is something that forms a part of your identity. The easiest way out of this is not to be proud because it is like a drop of poison in fresh milk. No matter how sweet the milk is, it is still deadly. Teach yourself humility and the first impression people have about you shall last longer, maybe eternally.

4. Poor hygiene.

You can never substitute hygiene with anything else. Imagine meeting this perfect person and then discovering their poor hygiene. It is a complete turn-off. It rolls back the impression you had about them and you see them in a new light. It is as if your eyes have been opened to something new.Sanitation is not a gender responsibility but a duty to every sane person. You can avoid the death of a good first impression by being clean throughout. Adopt a new mantra in your life that cleanliness is next to godliness.

5. Bad etiquette.

It is generally the absence of good social behavior for example talking with your mouth full, not greeting your elders, being impolite to attendants, among many more. At first sight, it is impossible to know somebody's etiquette until you spend some time with them. The high esteem you regarded a handsome young man or beautiful young lady immediately dies when you learn of their bad etiquette. Make good manners a part of your personality and you will not have trouble maintaining the good first impression you have on people.

Conclusion

Are you wondering what happened after meeting a prospective employer? Or maybe you wonder why you cannot maintain the good first impression you had on people. These are the top five killers of the first impression. There is no turning back once you work on them successfully.

Chapter 31:

10 Habits Of The Sigma Male

The sigma male has particular traits that distinguish them from alpha and beta males. He is an independent, successful, and self-made man who has created space for himself to thrive in a competitive world. Here are ten habits of the sigma male:

1. They Have Few Friends

Unlike the alpha, sigma males are not very social. They maintain a small circle of friends with whom they mingle freely. They are cautiously social and trust very few people with their issues.

They are neither introverts nor anti-social but have some degree of socialization that works in their favor. They are not great influencers but their opinions are highly valued.

2. They Live An Authentic Lifestyle

Sigma males are not people pleasers. They live genuinely lifestyles according to their financial ability and do not strain to outdo themselves regardless of whatever pressure is exerted on them.

Authenticity is an indelible mark in their lives. Sigma males have mastered the art of postponing unnecessary activities they cannot currently afford.

3. They Are Independent Of The Opinions Of Other People

Sigma males are unaffected by the opinions of other people about them. They are strong-willed and have developed a thick skin against harsh criticism.

Sigma males do not ignore correction. They are receptive to genuine opinions from other people and work on them to improve their image. Their independence of opinions from other people is to the extent that they are not easily influenced.

4. They Are Risk-Takers

Unlike beta males who prefer low risk in calm environments, sigma males have a higher risk appetite than them but lower than alpha males. They are ready to work themselves out in exchange for a small degree of risk.

Sigma males are afraid of risking much. Their fear of losing outweighs their ambition of gaining and they would rather take a longer route with medium or low risk rather than a shorter route with high risk.

5. They Are Self-Conscious

Sigma males are more self-aware of themselves. They know their limits, strengths, and weaknesses. They have conquered the battle on self-awareness and only handle what they know they can manage.

The self-consciousness of sigma males makes them successful in what they choose because they understand their level and their breaking points.

6. They Are Less Aggressive In Pursuing Their Dreams But Follow Them Nonetheless

Sigma males like the alpha males are visionary and focused on their goals. The distinction between them is that sigma males are less aggressive and can make a few compromises when the situation demands.

They are relentless in following their passion but their breaking point reaches sooner than expected. They have a clearly defined line on what they can and cannot do.

7. They Are Flexible

Sigma males are not rigid. They have room for any necessary adjustmentsto their plans. Their flexibility is admirable because they can easily fit in any situation. None of their plans is cast on stone.

The flexibility of sigma males should not be mistaken for lack of decisiveness. They are decisive and well-guided in their decisions. What makes them stand out is that they are open to necessary change, unlike alpha males who nothing can dissuade them once they are focused on their goals.

8. They Tend To Overthink

Sigma males often overthink even on simple issues. They are largely concerned about the ripple effect of their decisions on their lives and loved ones. To them, everything requires a complex solution.

Their overthinking does not mean they are indecisive but that they take longer to make decisions. They cannot be entrusted with a position of responsibility in making accurate decisions within a short time.

9. They Defy Social Norms

Sigma males often defy social traditions. They do not follow the norms that are expected of them probably because they find alternatives during their overthinking sprees. Their defiance of social norms is not because they are rude but their unique characteristics make them stand out.

The personalities of sigma males areunique because they go against the tide of prevailing social norms at the moment. Their nonconformity to societal expectations is their most conspicuous habit.

10. They Value Their Privacy

Sigma males highly value their privacy.They guard it with every resource at their disposal. It is difficult for their matters to leak to people outside their circle if they have not permitted such.

Privacy is what defines sigma males. They are not secretive but simply private. Their privacy protects them from the invasion of their space by the public.

IN CONCLUSION, THESE TEN HABITS OF SIGMA MALES DISTINGUISH THEM FROM OTHER GROUPS. ALTHOUGH THEY COULD

Chapter 32:

Five Ways To Rid Yourself Of Distraction

Are You Distracted?

Are you? Maybe we should begin by understanding what distractions are. Anything that makes you no longer concentrate on your goals is a distraction.

It could be your mobile phone's incoming notifications that make you stop working and attend to it. It could also be your mind straying to other things other than what is at hand. Anything can be a distraction at any one point.

Even the King is not immune to distractions!

Distractions can cause poor performance at work or school. They are a costly affair. It can only get worse if enough is not done to stop it.

Consider a driver driving a bus on a busy highway ferrying over fifty passengers. What will happen if he is distracted from driving and pays attention to other things? The lives of all the passengers on board would be in danger.

How about a surgeon in the theatre operating on a patient? He/she risks the patient's life by being distracted.

Do not defend yourself that you are neither a doctor nor a driver. You must have at one point or another found yourself distracted. Nothing bad happened, right? Still, you are not safe from its disastrous effects.

You should stop being distracted early enough before it gets chronic. Here are five effective ways to rid yourself of distraction:

1. Have Many Short-Term Targets Instead Of Long-Term Ones.

It is good to have targets. It is even better to have a long-term focus on your target. However, how prone are you to distractions?

You are more likely to be distracted when you are focused on something far away in the future. Many things happen between now and the future that you may not have control over. You may end up shifting your attention to what is importantpresently and forget about your long-term goals.

To prevent this disconnection, break down your long-term goals into manageable short-term milestones. You will be able to meet your goals in portions and in the long run,have fully fulfilled your target.

2. Take Periodic Breaks.

Learning institutions have known this simple life hack. They give students periodic breaks. In a single day, some schools have two breaks, a lunch break, and even a games break towards the evening. This is not a waste of time.

Breaks have a psychological effect on those that observe them. It gives your mind a chance to relax after a heightened duration of stiff concentration. Your mind becomes fresh when you resume from a break. Nothing can easily distract you until the next break.

Similarly, take periodic breaks from your work. It will help you organize your mind before you resume your work. Breaks are necessary to rid yourself of distractions.

3. Be In A Serene Environment.

The reason why you are easily distracted could be because you are in a noisy environment. Who will not get distracted from their work if the environment is not calm? You are not an exception.

The reason why examination halls are quiet is to rid those taking exams from distractions. Banking halls and libraries are equally very calm. Nothing should interrupt the focus of those in such places for them to achieve optimal focus.

Similarly, try changing your environment and move to a calmer place. There is value in changing locations. You will rid yourself ofunnecessary distractions that are a nuisance to workflow.

4. Master The Art Of Deep Focus.

Nothing can ever interrupt someone who has adopted deep focus as a lifestyle. It is a lifestyle of calmness and mastery of your emotions.

Let nothing hijack your emotions when you are in the middle of an important session. You have the power to choose what controls you.

You lose it when you allow every excuse to interrupt what you were doing. Be principled to follow through with what you are doing to completion or until you take a break, whichever comes earlier.

5. Reward Yourself For Every Achievement.

When was the last time you rewarded yourself? When you reward yourself for every goal you score, you will be motivated to remain focused on the upcoming goals so that you can be rewarded again.

It is normal for humans to want to be recognized and rewarded. The desire for such will rid you of distractions because you know once you stray no reward will be forthcoming.

These five ways are effective in ridding yourself of distractions.

Chapter 33:

How To Deal With Stress (For Women)

Stress is an inevitablepart of everyone's life, and it's no secret that stress wears on your emotions and wreaks havoc on your physical health. Women face unique challenges and have unique needs for stress management. The circumstances are that as a woman, you are juggling many responsibilities that you barely have time to manage stress;such that when you find yourself in a stressful situation, you handle it in an unhealthy way like overeating, drinking alcohol, or just laying around.

While it's almost impossible to do away with all the stress in your life, you can manage the situation and improve your health. A personalized care plan that includes time to recover and self-care can help you handle stress and motivate you to make healthier lifestyle choices. So how can you manage stress in your life?

Here is how to deal with stress.

1. Classify the Problem

First, classify the stressors in stressful situations rationally and how you responded to them. Keep a record of the events that caused your stress, including who was involved, the physical setting, and how you reacted. Taking notes can help you identify patterns in your stressors and reactions to them, allowing you to develop a stress management strategy.

2. Make Use of Mantras

Think of a mantra, and in this particular case, there are two effective ones; "I'm sure I can do it" or "That's not going to work for me." The former sentiment reminds you that you're capable of completing the task at hand. While the latter assures you that you are not always required to. Give your all to the things worth your time and effort, and let the rest go. You don't always have a choice, but when you do, it's okay to say no if saying yes will push you beyond your healthy limits.

3. Choose Your Battles

You don't always control external stressors, but you can practice restraint when it comes to internal stressors; that is the expectations you place on yourself. There's no reason trying to be all things to everyone and then feeling like a failure if you don't get to do everything.

4. Get Enough Sleep

A good night's sleep gives you a competitive advantage. Sleep is a form of self-care and one of the most effective ways to meet your physical, mental, and emotional needs. Giving up sleep is the same as giving up fuel. You get refueled after a good night's sleep, which helps you manage and reduce stress.

5. Figure a Way To Grow in the Challenge

Stress can cause you to think in a limited, pessimistic manner. However, this does not have to be the case all the time. Find your happy medium and calm those overwhelming or stressful thoughts. You'll probably become tolerant of stressors once you find a different approaching perspective.

6. Engage in a Physical Exercise

Exercising for your mental health doesn't have to be as rigorous as training for physical fitness. Almost any kind of regular exercise will get you there. Whatever type of exercise you choose, rest assured that it will lower stress hormones produced by your body while enhancing your mood-endorphins.

7. Chill Out a Bit

Unless you're in a life-or-death situation, a twenty-minute break won't hurt. Instead, take some time off and engage in things you enjoy doing. You can read, have a latte with a friend, or even enjoy your favorite show. Taking your mind off your problems reset your mind such that you return to them with a fresh perspective.

8. Get Organised

Nothing beats stress than being prepared and organised. It gives you a sense of control you may never imagine. Nothing exacerbates your stress like that piled-up paperwork, or a cluttered kitchen, or a backlog of emails. Set some time aside to address the issue or seek assistance.

9. Talk to Someone

Sometimes your problems become bigger when you keep everything to yourself. Get out, and talk to someone, be it a friend, or more so seeking professional help. Talking things out enables you to find solutions to your problems, thus triggering stress management.

Conclusion

Societal expectations are that a womanmustmultitaskand do everything expected of a "typical woman" in order to earn a place or be valued. Resist and do things on your own terms because once you conform to such expectations, you're opening an avenue for mental health issues. Don't let this strenuous and frazzled world get the best of you.

Chapter 34:

5 Signs You Are Smarter Than Most People

If you've been called smart or intelligent your whole life, it may be for any of the reasons listed below. That's according to science, of course. And if the verdict is still out on whether you're truly smart, this may just make your day. Perhaps you've been a genius in disguise the whole time. Well, not anymore

1. You Talk To Yourself

Have you ever been working really hard, and found yourself accidentally talking to yourself? If so, though it might be a sign of higher intelligence!

According to an article from Medical Daily, talking to yourself could be your brain's way of organizing the many thoughts that pop up . It could also be an extension of inner dialogue as you figure out how to navigate difficult or challenging tasks .

In any case, there seems to be a strong association between talking to yourself and success, and more studies suggest that this may not be a coincidence.

2. You Seem Lazy To Others

Do you like to spend more time in thought, or focused on a single thing? Have people called you lazy because of it? It turns out that this perceived laziness might be a sign that you are smarter than most people.

According to an article from The Indian Express, those with higher intelligence tend to stay immersed in their thoughts and curiosities for longer periods of time. This could lead to the appearance of boredom or laziness, when the exact opposite is actually happening.

3. You Work At Night

Are you a night owl? It turns out, this may be a trait of higher intelligence.

Though studies have shown that morning people are generally happier, research shows a correlation between being more productive at night and having higher intelligence, according to an article from Inc. by Jeff Haden. However, this isn't to say that there is a causation or proven fact.

When it comes to sleep, the most important things are to maintain a consistent schedule and get enough sleep each night. There are advantages and disadvantages to rising early and staying up late. As long as you listen to your body and do what is truly best for you, you're on your way to being the happiest and healthiest you can be!

4. You Are Artistically Inclined

Do you love painting, drawing, singing, or playing the violin? Being artistically inclined develops your brain like no other and can boost your intelligence.

Research suggests that there is a link between the arts and intelligence that is scattered throughout the brain, such as in areas responsible for memory, attention and others related to cognitive functioning. It turns out that many forms of art are also stress relievers. So every time you practice the piano or learn a TikTok dance, you're likely helping yourself out in more ways than one!

5. You Occasionally Procrastinate

Do you wait until the last minute to finish papers and projects? Procrastination, while not the best for time management, might be a sign that you are smarter than most people.

But, as Haden explains, there are caveats. He says that while studies do suggest that procrastination can fuel innovation, there is a difference between procrastinating to avoid working and procrastinating to come up with better ideas. This distinction is important—saving everything for the last minute will leave you stressed in the end and sadly won't contribute much to bolstering intelligence.

We hope you enjoyed learning about a few signs that you may be smarter than most people. Could you relate? Did we miss any? Thanks for reading!

www.ingramcontent.com/pod-product-compliance
Lightning Source LLC
Chambersburg PA
CBHW071125130526
44590CB00056B/2282